Catholic Spiritual Classics

*Introductions to Twelve Classics
of Christian Spirituality*

Mitch Finley

D1446421

Sheed & Ward

Sheed & Ward TM is a service of National Catholic Reporter Publishing, Inc.

Library of Congress Catalog Card Number: 86-63588

ISBN: 1-55612-058-3

Published by: Sheed & Ward
            115 E. Armour Blvd. P.O. Box 414292
            Kansas City, MO 64141-0281
            To order, call: (800) 821-7926

Contents

This book is dedicated to:
Brother Thomas Frey, C.S.C.,
and
Reverend Dominic Petrucci

Foreword

I am certainly familiar with the classics of western spirituality so I did not think I would be able to read through this book which is something of a primer on the subject. I was wrong. It surprised me to see how replete the book was with fresh insights and pieces of information that were unknown to me and that I gladly picked up for use in my own lectures.

Anthony DeMello, S.J.

Introduction

How to Read a Spiritual Classic

There is a groundswell of renewed interest today in the classic writings of Christian spirituality. Many people find in the classics timeless guidelines for their daily lives—a renewal of their commitment to gospel values, encouragement in prayer, and good counsel for their personal relationships.

A literary work becomes a Christian spiritual classic when, over long periods of time, countless readers find in that work special wisdom to help them live a Christian life. Although the list of spiritual classics is long, one quality tends to characterize them all. Each in a unique fashion echoes the challenge and comfort of the gospel; each takes seriously the central place in the believer's life of a dedication to love of God and neighbor. Each also takes seriously the need to reject whatever may obstruct that dedication. Each acknowledges that this commitment depends, in turn, on the ability to embrace life exactly as it is.

My existence may not be exactly what I would wish for, but it is my life, and it is here that God calls me to service, prayer, and joy. My life is the result of many choices, some made for me (wisely or unwisely) by others, some made (wisely or unwisely) by myself. Through them all God has been at work.

To the extent that I am able to speak a resounding "Yes!" to my life *as it is*, to that extent I am free to forget myself in loving service of God and other people. Most classics, following the lead of the gospel, take for granted this perspective.

This does not mean, of course, that I should stop trying to grow and deepen. Nor does it mean that I should give up trying to right injustices and otherwise improve the world around me. It means, rather, that I do not confuse my value in the eyes of other people, or in the eyes of a commercialized culture with my true value. I am called to say yes to myself, as I am with all my faults and limitations, gifts and talents, because I believe that God's love for me is unconditional. To say yes to myself and to my life is to say yes to God's love for me, to which there are no strings attached.

Keep the above in mind, for example, when reading Book 3, Chapter 8 of *The Imitation of Christ*, which is titled, "On thinking nothing of oneself in the sight of God." How easily such ideas may be misunderstood today! Thomas a Kempis did not want people literally to "despise" themselves, in the modern sense of the word. Rather, he simply wanted them to appreciate more deeply their complete dependence upon God.

Among the spiritual classics literary styles vary widely. There are letters, autobiographies, various kinds of theological discourse, commentaries on Scripture, poetry, homilies, personal journals, legendary stories, history, and even theological fantasy.

As with each book of the Bible, it's critical for the modern reader to remain aware of the specific literary character of the classic at hand, otherwise the author's intentions are easily lost, and the intended meaning can be distorted or missed completely. Each author meant to convey truth by means of a specific literary style.

St. John of the Cross' poetry must be read *as poetry*. Too, the reader must recall that this poetry is an attempt to describe the author's experience of contemplative prayer, so it's loaded with allegory and metaphor, without which the mystic is speechless.

The Way of a Pilgrim, the 19th-century journal of an anonymous Russian Orthodox pilgrim which teaches the popular "Jesus Prayer," should be read as part personal history, part inspirational fiction. *The Little Flowers of St. Francis*, though rooted in historical events, is for the most part a collection of charming legends about St. Francis and the earliest Franciscans. Both works, through their unique literary styles, teach truths of the spiritual life.

Along with the specific literary character of each classic, it is also important to keep in mind the effects of the years—sometimes centuries—which have passed since the author took pen in hand.

The Imitation of Christ, for example, was written in the early 1400s. Obviously, we live in a different world today. Not only may we measure our lives against the teachings of the *Imitation*, but the *Imitation* must be held up to the mirror of the present era to see how it fares. Thomas a Kempis, just as modern authors, had his blind spots and prejudices.

One of the most significant historical shifts that we must keep in mind when reading many classics relates to our understanding of human nature. Various pagan philosophies had an impact on the early Christians. Later (during the 17th and 18th centuries) the Jansenist heresy, though condemned by popes, had a profound effect on French and Irish piety especially, which in turn affected American Catholicism through countless French and Irish Catholic immigrants.

Both the ancient pagan philosophies and Jansenism lent perspectives to Christianity which, among other things, deeply distrusted human emotions and human sexuality. Jansenism misunderstood the writings of St. Augustine (who was affected by the Manichees who thought human sexuality evil), and adopted misinterpretations of St. Paul's distinction (in, for example, Romans 8) between the flesh and the spirit.

Jansenism was unaware that when St. Paul wrote about "the sins of the flesh," he meant far more than sexual sins. He was referring to any action—including economic injustice and gossiping—which would damage people's relationships with one another and with God. St. Paul followed Jesus in that sexual sins were rather far down his list of significant sins. The Jansenists, on the other hand, could think of nothing more horrible.

The late Msgr. Ronald Knox, in his own modern theological classic, *Enthusiasm*, pointed out the "semi-Jansenist atmosphere" in *The Imitation of Christ*. He might well have remarked on the same "atmosphere" in many other spiritual classics.

Today, in great part through what Old Testament scholar J. Coert Rylaarsdam calls "a subterranean reappropriation of our Jewish roots," we are regaining a sense of the goodness of human emotions and sexuality. As the creation narratives in the Book of Genesis teach, sexuality reveals the divine in the human, and male and female are meant to help one another draw closer to God.

The Bible's *Song of Songs*, though interpreted in other valid ways, is fundamentally a celebration of the goodness of sexual love.

For most modern theologians of the spiritual life, the bottom line is this: human beings are a unity, body and spirit together. What affects one affects the other. We are embodied spirits. Thus, sexual lovemaking is simultaneously one of the most bodily and most spiritual events in a Christian marriage.

To attempt to hold one's sexuality at arm's length is to distort or cripple one's spirituality. To neglect prayer is to deprive oneself spiritually, psychologically, emotionally, and biologically. To truly despise myself, or to cling to self-defeating behaviors (which include overeating, drug abuse, and mental name-calling—such as calling myself an idiot when I make a mistake) does as much spiritual harm as psychological and physiological damage.

Another perspective present in many classics is a tendency that *seems* to recommend a spirituality which is individualistic or privatized. We certainly need a greater appreciation today for the value of solitude in the Christian life. But, as Matthew 25 teaches in the parable of the sheep and the goats, there is something of ultimate value about caring human relationships. Love of God and love of other people are inseparable. "Whoever does not love the brother whom he can see," says the First Letter of John (4:20), "cannot love God whom he has not seen."

To nourish oneself spiritually through prayer, reading, and meditation, interpersonally through family, friendship, and serving others, and physically through nutritious food, regular exercise, and enough sleep, is to "get one's act together" on all levels.

A balanced spirituality results in a whole Christian lifestyle. That is, it conditions every dimension of life. It is also fully Christian to the extent that each of its aspects becomes a way to forget oneself for the sake of God and other people.

The Little Flowers of St. Francis holds up for emulation Brother Peregrine, who "very rarely visited his blood relations. He would encourage them to despise the world and with serious words urge them to the love of God; then hurriedly and hastily he would withdraw from them saying that Jesus Christ who ennobles the soul, is not to be found among relatives and acquaintances."

Sorry, Brother Peregrine, but there is little that's Christian about such an attitude. A balanced spirituality may take such words as cautions against an overemphasis on one dimension of a Christian spirituality to the neglect of the others.

Cultural differences are important, too. As recently as the early 1960s, for example, when Thomas Merton published his modern classic, *New Seeds of Contemplation*, it was culturally acceptable for writers to use almost exclusively male references. Today, many people are uncomfortable with the use of the words "man," "he," and "him" to refer to both the male and female members of humankind. Though it's sometimes more cumbersome stylistically, today our culture is weighted in favor of those who prefer more inclusive language. It is unfair, of course, to expect such sensitivities from the authors of the classics. They were as time- and culture-bound as we.

No classic was written yesterday. Just as Scripture should not be read uncritically, neither should a spiritual classic be read uncritically. To benefit most fully from its wisdom, a classic requires an informed and intelligent reading. It's important to read *about* the classic before reading the classic itself.

The classics of Christian spirituality have stood the test of time. Along with the teachings of the church, the lives of the saints, the history of theological reflection, many cultural embodiments of

Christian piety, the liturgical tradition, and modern forms of spirituality, the classics belong to Sacred Tradition. They are there to teach
us, to be treasured as deep wells from which to draw living water.

This book discusses twelve classics of Christian spirituality. There
has been no attempt at original scholarship, no attempt to present
an exhaustive introduction to each classic chosen. Rather, this
book's purpose is to offer a lively thumbnail sketch of each one.
Each chapter includes also a short reflection on ways that particular classic might apply to contemporary Christian living.

Those who wish to read an original classic will find here enough
information upon which to base a selection. Those who want simply to know something about some of the classics may gain accurate
insights into the spirit and flavor of the individual works.

There is no intention here to summarize every aspect of the classics discussed. Rather, each chapter confines itself to the fundamental themes in the work it discusses. Introductions to spiritual classics,
in an attempt to be thorough, sometimes end up boring their readers
half to death. It is the author's fondest wish to have avoided such
writing in this book.

There are many, many classics of Christian spirituality. By no
means are the ones included here necessarily the most important.
It seems to the author, however, that most people are more likely
to read classics that are of manageable length and of a less erudite
nature. Thus, for all their value, not included are the 16th-century
works of St. John of the Cross and St. Teresa of Avila. Boethius' *Consolation of Philosophy* seemed too abstruse for most people, including the author, as did Pascal's *Pensees*. Because of their technical
nature, also not included are the *Summa* of St. Thomas Aquinas,
and Cardinal Newman's *Apologia Pro Vita Sua* and *On the Development of Christian Doctrine*.

On the other hand, some classics that might have been included
were passed by simply due to a need to draw the line someplace.
This list includes *The Little Flowers of St. Francis*, and G.K. Chester-
ton's masterpieces, *Orthodoxy* and *St. Francis of Assisi*. Among the
modern classics not included is Thomas Merton's famous 1948

autobiography, *The Seven Storey Mountain*, but this needs little introduction and is easily available to anyone who wants to read it.

The only work discussed here that may well require outside assistance in order to plumb its depths is Dante's *Divine Comedy*. (The same may be said about the last few chapters of St. Augustine's *Confessions*, but the rest of the book is easily read.) Dante's classic is here all the same, because it has the unique distinction of being not only the greatest work of poetry ever written, but also the greatest work of theological fantasy ever written.

It is evident in several of the essays that make up this book that the author owes a debt of thanks to various scholars upon whose work he gladly relied. The author thanks these scholars for the help they provided through their research and writing.

If the reader finds here some help in applying the insights of one or more of these twelve classics to his or her own life, this book's purpose will have been accomplished.

The author dedicates this book to Brother Thomas Frey, C.S.C., and Father Dominic Petrucci—two kind and dedicated guides along the path of Christian faith.

1
Thomas a Kempis'
The Imitation Of Christ

The Imitation of Christ is sometimes called the most widely read book in the world, after the Bible. As a seminarian, the future Pope John XXIII copied down excerpts from it in his private journal. Dorothy Day wrote that it "followed me through my days. Again and again I came across copies of it and the reading of it brought me comfort." Bramachari, a Hindu monk, advised the young Thomas Merton to read it.

The *Imitation*'s exact date of publication is impossible to determine, but scholars agree that it was in circulation by the year 1427, and popular throughout Western Europe. Originally written in Latin, it was soon translated into Dutch, German, French, English and Italian. Printed editions appeared toward the end of the 1400s.

Today, eighteen English editions appear in *Books in Print*. There are large print, Braille, and audio cassette editions for the visually handicapped.

Since its appearance over five hundred years ago, some thirty-five different people have been suggested as author of the *Imita-*

tion. Most scholars, however, vote for the traditional author, Thomas a Kempis.

Thomas Haemerken, born in Kempen, the Rhineland, in 1379 or 1380, was the second son of John and Gertrude Haemerken. Though they were peasants, the Haemerkens managed to send Thomas to schools in Deventer, which were operated by the Brothers of the Common Life, a community of lay people and some priests. Thomas thought he would join the Brothers of the Common Life, but in 1399 he chose instead a newly founded monastery of the Canons Regular of St. Augustine, in Zwolle, the Netherlands. His older brother, John, was prior there.

Little is known of Thomas' activities in the monastery at Mount St. Agnes, except that he copied manuscripts and composed numerous works, including some lives of the saints. Twice he served as subprior, and for a time was master of novices. Thomas died on August 8, 1471, in the monastery where he had spent virtually his entire adult life.

Thomas a Kempis relied on many sources in writing *The Imitation of Christ*. About one thousand direct and indirect quotations from the Bible have been identified, as well as numerous unacknowledged "borrowings" from masters of the spiritual life, including St. Bernard of Clairvaux, William of St. Thierry, and *The Cloud of Unknowing*. Most directly, however, the *Imitation* is rooted in a spiritual renewal movement, the Devotio Moderna, which appeared in Western Europe in the last decades of the fifteenth century.

This was one of the darkest periods in the church's history, a time of corrupt faith among both laity and clergy. Into this darkness the light of the Devotio Moderna shone brightly during the century just prior to the birth of Martin Luther (1483). "However much it is necessary to describe the inefficiency, the arbitrariness, the laxity and injustice of parish life under the fattened and sluggish clericalism of the time," wrote Martin Marty, in *A Short History of Christianity*, "it is necessary again and again to stress that the holiness of the church still found a front against the world in the common life of the people. . . . Few better examples of this residue of holiness survive in Christian memory than that of the Brotherhood of the Common Life, which flourished in the Low Countries in late medieval times."

The Imitation of Christ is rooted in the Devotio Moderna as it was lived by the Brothers of the Common Life. Thomas a Kempis became a priest, but he spent his early years in schools operated by the Brothers. And the Augustinian community he joined was a direct spin-off of this same tradition. Thomas "called all to serious pursuit of the path Christ had walked," says Martin Marty, "in marked contradiction of their times."

The *Imitation* consists of four separate books, only the first of which was originally titled *De Imitatione Christi*. In Book 1, Thomas reflects on the problems and temptations to be expected in the early stages of the spiritual life. The theme of separation from the world—appropriate to a monastic vocation—dominates, and Thomas emphasizes the need to follow the example of Christ.

Book 2 is quieter in tone, with more emphasis on the peace to be gained from a detachment from external events. Thomas turns over and over to the inner joy to be found through faith. But this inner peace cannot be obtained apart from sacrifice and the cross, writes Thomas, and so Christians must expect the pain of self-denial and the discomfort of discipline.

In Book 3 the author's style shifts to one of dialogue between "the Disciple" and "the Voice of the Lord." Spiritual comfort is the main theme. The spirit of humility and self-effacement is uppermost. Conscious of his own "nothingness," the disciple is even more aware of the love of the Lord who cares for him in spite of his unworthiness.

The final book of the *Imitation* has the greatest internal unity, due to its single theme—"A Reverent Recommendation to Holy Communion." Now the divine name is "Dilectus," the Beloved. The eucharistic bread is a sacramental medicine, "the health of soul and body, the remedy for every sickness of the spirit," and an object of worship.

Betty I. Knott, in her Introduction to the Collins edition, wrote: "[*The Imitation of Christ*] is a distillation of the atmosphere, beliefs, and ideals of a whole religious movement—the mysticism and piety of the Netherlands and Rhineland in the 14th and 15th centuries..."

Because the *Imitation* is a product of a culture and an age long dead, it makes special demands on the modern reader who should remember the historical and religious contexts from which the *Imitation* emerged. It is also prudent to be on the lookout for manifestations of simple human shortsightedness. The fifteenth century, no less than the twentieth, had its limitations as well as it virtues.

In his 1950 classic, *Enthusiasm*, Msgr. Ronald Knox remarked on "the semi-Jansenist atmosphere" of the *Imitation*, "which escapes so many readers." For Thomas a Kempis, "the world" and "the things of the world" are first of all a danger to the spiritual life. He never takes quite seriously the impact of the Incarnation and Redemption on the created order and human societies. Neither should he be expected to do so, since this was not a characteristic of theological perspectives and piety of his time.

The Eucharistic spirituality of Book 4 comes from a time when believers had long forgotten the ways in which the Eucharist was understood and celebrated by the apostles and the early church. For Thomas a Kempis, the eucharistic bread is primarily a remedy for spiritual ills and an object to worship. Gone is the (at least) equally important truth, which the early church took for granted, that the Eucharist is a communal sharing of the Body and Blood (that is, the whole person) of the risen Christ.

Thomas a Kempis is sometimes quoted to support anti- intellectualism. One of the most famous passages from the *Imitation* is this one: "I would rather be able to feel compunction in my heart than be able to define it."

But remember that Thomas was trained in the Devotio Moderna, a tradition that placed much value on the intellect and academic studies. Famous lines like, "Learned arguments do not make a man holy . . ." take for granted the goodness of intellectual pursuits, but caution the reader to guard against academics divorced from the love of God and neighbor.

The Imitation of Christ presents a spirituality that developed in the midst of religious laxity and ecclesiastical corruption. Perhaps if the Devotio Moderna could have had a wider impact on the world of its time Martin Luther would have remained an obscure Augustinian monk.

The first words of the *Imitation* are perhaps its most important; surely they remain as central to the Christian life as ever:

> "He who follows me can never walk in darkness, says the Lord. By these words Christ urges us to mold our lives and characters in the image of his . . . Let us therefore see that we endeavor beyond all else to meditate on the life of Jesus Christ."

Contemporary Application

In recent decades *The Imitation of Christ* has been neglected by many as an embodiment of a spirituality inappropriate to contemporary concerns. Yet its core message—the need to "imitate Christ"—is timeless.

The idea, of course, is not to adopt a literal imitation of Christ, even if enough information were available about the life of the historical Jesus to do so. Rather, the idea is to become so subject to the guidance of the Holy Spirit as to reflect in one's own ordinary life Christ present in the world—to become an *alter Christus*, another Christ.

The *Imitation* encourages separation from the world. This makes perfect sense today, if understood simply to recommend an embracing of the Gospel which, unavoidably, sometimes places one at odds with the values and goals of society at large. Indeed, this emotional and spiritual ''separation'' is a basic source of the freedom necessary to a Christian life.

Peace of mind and heart is essential, says the *Imitation*. Yet sacrifices are necessary to gain this peace. Instead of the ''peace'' that the world offers—through the drug-like effects of heavy television-watching, and through the spirit-numbing pleasures of a lifestyle based on consumerism—instead, seek the peace only Christ can give, the peace that comes through a life dominated by love of God and neighbor.

2
St. Augustine's Confessions

In the intellectual history of Catholic Christianity two figures stand above the rest: St. Augustine of Hippo (354-430), and St. Thomas Aquinas (c. 1225-1274). Which to rank first? Many would give Thomas the edge. All the same, in some respects Thomas stood on Augustine's shoulders, and St. Augustine retains the distinction of having written one of the greatest autobiographies in the history of Western civilization: the *Confessions*.

Augustine was born November 13, 354, in Tagaste, northern Africa, near the eastern border of modern Algeria. The son of Patricius, a Roman official unsympathetic to Christianity, and Monica, a Christian, Augustine received a Christian upbringing. It was not the custom, however, to baptize infants.

Augustine's early goal was to become a lawyer, but he turned to literary pursuits after beginning studies in 370 at the university at Carthage. During this time he gradually gave up the Christian faith, and began living with a woman whose name is unknown, to whom he was faithful for fourteen years. A son, Adeodatus, was born in 372.

In 373 Augustine converted to Manichaeism, an extremely popular pseudo-Christian sect which taught the equal power and reality of good and evil. The Manichees proclaimed that the human body was evil, rejected the Old Testament, attacked the New Testament, and offered rational solutions to the problems of life.

Augustine became a teacher, and in 384 accepted the chair of rhetoric in Milan. It was here that he met Bishop Ambrose, and began listening to the famous preacher's sermons. The sermons were highly instrumental in Augustine's conversion to Christianity.

In the *Confessions* Augustine describes the event which finally led to his change of heart. Hearing the voice of a child chanting, "Take up and read. Take up and read," Augustine read from a book of the Gospels and then from one of St. Paul's letters. "Instantly," writes Augustine, ". . . as if before a peaceful light streaming into my heart, all the dark shadows of doubt fled away."

Baptized on Easter Eve, 387, the next year Augustine founded a quasi-monastic community in Tagaste. His reputation spread, however, and in 391 he was virtually dragged off by the people of nearby Hippo and ordained a priest. Soon Augustine gained a reputation for his preaching. In 395 he was made coadjutor to the aged Bishop Valerius of Hippo and, upon the old bishop's death, succeeded him the following year. About two years later, Augustine began dictating the *Confessions*.

Augustine wrote his spiritual and intellectual autobiography as he was entering middle age. Peter Brown, perhaps Augustine's greatest modern biographer, describes the *Confessions* as "not a book of reminiscences," but "an anxious turning to the past," a "poignant book," and "an act of therapy." "The book," asserts Brown, "owes its lasting appeal to the way in which Augustine, in his middle-age, had dared to open himself up to the feelings of his youth."

The *Confessions* reflect both continuity with literary styles of Augustine's time, and a radical innovation. Augustine, says Brown, writes his "prolonged exploration of the nature of God . . . in the form of a prayer," a style common to religious philosophers of the fourth century. But never before had anyone used this style "to strike up a lively conversation" with God. Philosophers of Augustine's time, wrote E. R. Dodds, "never gossiped with the One as Augustine gossips in the *Confessions*." Thus, Augustine's masterpiece startled his contemporaries.

Thirteen books make up the *Confessions*. Augustine includes discussions of his own character, events from his life, examinations of philosophical problems, a theory of time, a natural theology, and a metaphysics of being. Augustine also turns his attention to the nature of memory, the relation between sense and intellect, and the freedom of the will. The divinity and humanity of Christ, the Church as Christ's mystical body, the sacraments, grace, and prayer, also are featured in Augustine's self-revelation. Lest all this should sound overwhelming, however, Peter Brown reminds us that, "Augustine communicates such a sense of intense personal involvement in the ideas he is handling, that we are made to forget that it is an exceptionally difficult book."

In Books 1-9 Augustine tells his story from his birth to the time of his conversion and the death of Monica, his mother. This covers the first thirty-three years of the author's life. Book 1 contains the famous words which, says John K. Ryan in the Introduction to his translation of the *Confessions*, "sum up Augustine's whole teaching on man's relation to God:" ". . . you have made us for yourself, and our heart is restless until it rests in you."

Augustine turns in Book 10 to the present in which he was writing, and an examination of contemporary issues. He also provides a masterful analysis of human memory, and a psychological discussion of the human desire for happiness. "This is the happy life," writes Augustine in a passage which reveals his unwillingness to think in simplistic terms, "to rejoice over you, to you, and because of you: this it is, and there is no other. Those who think that there is another life pursue another joy and it is not true joy. Yet their will is not turned away from a certain image of joy."

The final three books of the *Confessions* are the most elaborate. Augustine dives into a meditation on time, eternity, and the created universe. "These things we see," he writes echoing Genesis, "and we see that each of them is good, and that all of them together are very good."

There is much that is timeless about the *Confessions*. St. Augustine reveals deep insights into human nature when he teaches that, in the words of Peter Brown, "A man cannot hope to find God unless he first finds himself . . . Above all, it is man's tragedy that he should be driven to flee 'outwards,' to lose touch with himself, to 'wander far' from his 'own heart.' "

Augustine by no means abandoned all he had learned from the "pagan" Greek philosophers. There is, for example, much evidence in the *Confessions* of Augustine's reliance on such philosophical works as the *Enneads* of Plotinus. Thus, some eight centuries later Thomas Aquinas was far from original when he used Aristotle as a foundation for his theological reflections. Modern theologians follow in the footsteps of Augustine and Thomas when they dialogue with the secular philosophies of our own time.

As with any book written centuries ago, it is wise to make allowances for the author's personal set of cultural and historical limitations. For example, though he rejected the Manichees and their good/evil, body/soul dualism, from a late 20th-century perspective Augustine seems still rather heavily affected by it. For Augustine, dealing with human sexuality is above all like walking on eggs. "Augustine, however," writes Peter Brown, "treats [his sexual sins] as not very important: in his eyes they paled into insignificance before a single act of vandalism."

Ten centuries after Augustine, Martin Luther was heavily influenced by his writings on the radical "fallenness" of human nature, a direction Thomas Aquinas had been reluctant to follow.

For all his reservations about humanity, however, Augustine was endless in his praise of God's creation. In one of his sermons he refers to "this smiling world." He was a man in love with God, a man devoted to his friends. "He is, above all," wrote Anne Fremantle, "the saint . . . who enjoyed *everything* . . . . Augustine celebrated, in all his works, the beauty and the reality of creation reflecting its Creator."

The *Confessions* of St. Augustine retain their attraction for thoughtful people because they embody insights into life, the world, and relationships with God and other people. Late in life, at the age of seventy-four, Augustine reassessed his writings and had this to say about the *Confessions*: ". . . they still move me, when I read them now, as they moved me when I first wrote them."

For nearly 1,600 years countless readers have felt the same.

Contemporary Application

When St. Augustine wrote his *Confessions* he did something no one in history had ever done before, simple though it seems today. He wrote about himself in the first person. Essentially, what he did was turn to his own experience as a source of revelation. He listened to his own history to see what God had been saying there.

Anyone can do the same. To listen to one's own life, perhaps by keeping a journal, is one of the best ways to become more in touch with God present in the ordinary events that make up any life.

We tend to act as if God is present only in special moments, moments of prayer or solitude, events identified as officially sacred, such as the liturgy, or in times of quiet reflection. We forget, unless we take time to reflect, that God is present in the most casual occurrences. God is present in our work, in our recreation, and in our leisure. Above all, God is present in our relationships with other people.

Time after time in his *Confessions* Augustine recognized God at work in his personal relationships. We can do the same by recognizing that to make time to be with family and friends, simply to enjoy their company, and to serve those with special needs, is to draw close to God, as well.

3
Julian of Norwich's *Showings*

Readers of T. S. Eliot's *Four Quartets* often think they tap original work when they come to the section of "Little Gidding" where Eliot wrote, "Sin is Behovely, but / All shall be well, and / All manner of thing shall be well."

In "East Coker," Eliot uses images from St. John of the Cross. But did the poet not draw from his own well in "Burnt Norton" when he used the image, "the still point of the turning world?"

On the contrary. T. S. Eliot was an admirer of and—in *Four Quartets*—a borrower from a woman known as Julian of Norwich. Though Julian's writings were discovered in 1902, it is only in the last decade that she has attracted the attention she deserves.

In her Foreword to Brendan Doyle's *Meditations With Julian of Norwich*, Julian scholar Patricia Vinje writes: "Very little is known about the person who wrote these meditations and reflections, not even the author's name. . . On May 13, 1373, when she was thirty and a half years old, she reported seeing sixteen showings, or mystical visions. Quite soon after this event the young woman recorded the content of these revelations in a text entitled *A Book of Showings*. Some fifteen to twenty years later, she produced an extended version of the same sixteen revelations."

The woman known as Julian took her name, as was the anchoritic custom, from the church to which her anchorhold, or cell, was attached: the Church of St. Julian at Norwich, in East Anglia, England. No one knows whether she adopted the anchoritic lifestyle before or after she wrote the later edition of the *Book of Showings*. Civil records of Norwich, however, suggest that the Lady Julian remained in her cell until her death sometime between 1416 and 1419.

In the Prologue to his delightful two-act play, *Julian*, Jesuit Father J. Janda says: "[Julian] was an anchoress, that is, a woman who chose a life of solitude and prayer, and lived in a small two-room apartment adjoining a church. An anchoress was not necessarily a nun."

Dame Julian's anchorhold had one window, into the church, through which she could assist at Mass and receive Communion, and another window through which she received those who came seeking advice and counsel. Father Janda places these words on Julian's lips: "So many come— / for spiritual advice / or ghostly counsel, / as they say; / they speak of / pain and loss, / confusion and despair, / fear and death, / the sorrowing, / the sick, / the unwanted, / the lonely, / both young and old, / rich and poor, / all come to my window. / 'No one listens,' they tell me, / and so I listen / and tell them / what they have just / told me, / and I sit in silence / listening to them, / letting them grieve. / 'Julian, you are wise,' / they say, / 'you have been gifted / with understanding.' / All I did was listen."

Newcomers to Julian of Norwich, you're in for the treat of your life. Whether you choose to read the complete work, Brendan Doyle's refreshingly contemporary translation of excerpts (mentioned above), or a more traditional translation of selections like

Enfolded in Love: Daily Readings with Julian of Norwich, Dame Julian may well knock your spiritual socks off.

The dominant theme in Julian's writings may be her emphasis on the goodness of God and the goodness of Creation. "God is goodness . . . God is nothing but goodness," she writes. "God is everything which is good, as I see it, and the goodness which everything has is God." Julian is thrilled with the goodness of humanity, commenting on "our noble and excellent making." God, says Julian, is "delighting without end" over the goodness and beauty of the human person, which is "as beautiful, as good, as precious a creature as God could make."

Among the most famous of Julian's words are these: "God showed me in my palm a little thing round as a ball about the size of a hazelnut. I looked at it with the eye of my understanding and asked myself, 'What is this thing?' And I was answered: 'It is everything that is created.' I wondered how it could survive since it seemed so little it could suddenly disintegrate into nothing. The answer came: 'It endures and ever will endure, because God loves it.' And so everything has being because of God's love."

Julian praises the relationship between body and soul, which, she says, forms a "glorious union." Body and soul are to be on friendly terms. "Let each of them take help from the other," she writes.

Julian identifies the soul with sensuality. "As regards our sensuality," writes the anchoress of Norwich, "it can rightly be called our soul because of the union it has with God."

Salvation, for Julian of Norwich, is not so much a matter of being saved from original sin. The Incarnation, she says, is meant to heal the two sides of human nature. "Just as in Christ two natures are united," writes Father Matthew Fox in his Preface to *Meditations With Julian of Norwich* "—the divine and the human—so too are we to become whole and healed."

Julian of Norwich is well known for her emphasis on the theme of the motherhood of God. The anchoress attributes motherhood to God, to Christ, to the Trinity, and to the Church.

"As we know, our own mother bore us only into pain and dying," says Lady Julian. "But our true mother Jesus, who is all love, bears us into joy and endless living . . . . A mother feeds her child with her milk, but our beloved mother Jesus feeds us with himself. In tender courtesy he gives us the Blessed Sacrament . . ." "Just as God is truly our Father," exclaims Dame Julian, "so also is God truly our Mother."

In Father Janda's play, Julian remarks to her visitor, Margery Kempe, a mystic herself, that she would never use feminine images for God "to confuse / a priest or bishop—/ only to women such as we—/ Yes. That is our joke."

The intimate relationship between God and humanity is another of Julian's themes. "We are of God," she writes. "That is what we are. I saw no difference between God and our substance but as if it were all God." Note, however, that Julian does *not* say that we are God, for, she says, "our substance is in God: that is, God is God, and our substance is a creature in God." For Julian, we are in God and God is in us.

Lady Julian's attitude toward sin is nothing if not startling. But the more you think about it, the more sense it makes, the more it seems to fit with a God who is love: "God said: 'It is necessary that sin should exist. But all shall be well, and all shall be well, and all manner of thing shall be well.' "

"God is our friend," says Julian, "who keeps us tenderly while we are in sin, and touches us privately, showing us where we went wrong by the sweet light of compassion and grace, even though we imagine that we will be punished."

The wisdom Lady Julian gained from many years of listening to other people's troubles—she lived to be seventy-four—has a disarming depth and simplicity. "God," she writes, "does not want us to be burdened because of sorrows and tempests that happen in our lives, because it has always been so before miracles happen."

Julian constantly urges her reader to trust in God, but in a way so captivating the reader can't help but feel affection for one who speaks with such authentic humility. "Often our trust is not full," she writes. "We are not certain that God hears us because we consider ourselves worthless and as nothing. This is ridiculous and the cause of our weakness. I have felt this way myself."

In the end, Julian's words usher the believer into eternity: "In heaven we shall see truly and everlastingly that we have grievously sinned in this life; notwithstanding we shall see that this in no way diminished His love, nor made us less precious in His sight."

In truth, says Lady Julian, "all shall be well, and all shall be well, and all manner of thing shall be well."

Contemporary Application

Julian of Norwich's habit of using feminine images for God is one that can nourish anyone's spiritual life today. Men can grow in their capacity to appreciate the feminine dimensions of life and the world by using feminine images of God in prayer. Unconscious tendencies to patronize women or fail to respect women as fully human can be neutralized by praying to a God who is Mother as well as Father, Lover as well as Unmoved Mover. Women can balance the ways masculine images of God have influenced them over a lifetime by doing the same.

If Father Janda's Julian character is authentic, Julian had a great gift for listening. People felt healed by being truly listened to. Experts on interpersonal communication insist that without the ability to listen no real communication can happen. How many marriages end in divorce simply because spouses no longer listen to one another?

Yet listening means more than not talking. Truly to listen is to become a well of quiet into which the other may pour himself or herself. The most effective listeners are people who regularly spend time in silence and solitude, even if only a few minutes a day. Something about listening to God, in the Scriptures, in meditative prayer, makes us able to listen to one another in ways that bring healing and wholeness.

4
The Cloud of Unknowing

If authentic Christian mysticism has to do with anything, it relates to the real world and real people, especially human relationships. "One of the greatest paradoxes of the mystical life," wrote Thomas Merton, "is this: that a man cannot enter into the deepest center of himself and pass through that center into God, unless he is able to pass entirely out of himself and empty himself and give himself to other people in the purity of a selfless love."

Some scholars believe that the author of the late 14thcentury spiritual classic, *The Cloud of Unknowing,* was a Carthusian monk and priest. At any rate, whoever wrote this masterpiece took for granted the understanding of mysticism articulated 600 years later by Thomas Merton. The anonymous author knew that love of God and love for other people are, for Christians, inseparable.

The Cloud of Unknowing teaches a method of contemplative prayer that is at once practical, based on authentic Christian tradition, and deeply rooted in the author's time and place. Dominican Father Simon Tugwell calls it "one of the gems of medieval English literature," and reminds the reader that the *Cloud* "must be interpreted primarily with reference to contemporary [that is, 14th century] sources and concerns."

Thus, *The Cloud of Unknowing* sometimes seems to drive a wedge between body and soul, mind and spirit. The author at times seems to suggest that "the flesh" is highly suspect, that true spirituality scorns the body. Such an attitude can only be viewed as un-Christian, and can result in a spirituality that leaves God's creation behind—which, for a religion based on Incarnation, is sheer nonsense.

Really, this is not what the author of *The Cloud of Unknowing* teaches. But it is easy to misunderstand him. A precise reading is necessary. When the author writes, says Father Tugwell, that during prayer there should be no thought of "created things," that is exactly what he means: there should be no *thought* of created things. He does not mean that God's creation is bad. The key to understanding *The Cloud of Unknowing*, in fact, is the knowledge that love is what both life and contemplative prayer are all about.

The author of *The Cloud* is quite explicit about his understanding of human nature. Says he: "God forbid that I should separate body and spirit when God has made them a unity."

The Cloud of Unknowing begins with a cautionary note. No one is to read this book unless that person is "deeply committed to follow Christ perfectly." This book is only for those who have proven themselves "for some time" faithful to "the active life," that is, to active loving service of others; "otherwise [they] will not be prepared to fathom the contents of this book." Thus the author does an end run on anyone so naive as to think that contemplative prayer is a legitimate way to tiptoe around the sacrifices required of Christians in the knockabout world, and the need for faithfulness to human relationships.

The way to begin contemplative prayer, says *The Cloud*, is to "lift up your heart to the Lord . . . Center all your attention and desire

on him and let this be the sole concern of your mind and heart."
Remember, however, that contemplative prayer is hard work. You
should persevere "until you feel joy in it."

In the beginning, however, "it is usual to feel nothing but a kind
of darkness about your mind, or as it were, a *cloud of unknowing.*"
This is the normal condition of contemplative prayer. "For if . . . you
hope to feel and see God as he is in himself it must be within this
darkness and this cloud." The author says, however, that he is sure
that to anyone who is patient "God in his goodness will bring you
to a deep experience of himself."

The basic method of prayer taught here is a simple one. In order
to pursue this contemplative prayer, it is essential to forget everything else during the time of prayer. You must abandon all "beneath
the cloud of forgetting."

Choose a single word, says *The Cloud,* such as "God," and repeat
this one word over and over in your heart during the time of prayer.
Continue to be patient with the cloud of unknowing above, and the
cloud of forgetting below.

Along with all the great mystics, however, the author of *The Cloud
of Unknowing* insists that contemplative prayer is a gift, that no one
can experience true contemplative prayer through human efforts
alone. "I am trying to make clear with words," he writes, "what
experience teaches more convincingly, that techniques and
methods are ultimately useless for awakening contemplative love."

Do not be irritated by those who say that contemplative prayer
is useless, and remember that "those who are perfectly humble will
lack nothing they really need, either spiritually or materially."

The Cloud of Unknowing is loaded with practical spiritual guidelines that are helpful for anyone. ". . . think twice about passing
judgment on the lives of other men. In the privacy of your own conscience judge yourself as you see fit before God or before your
spiritual father, but do not meddle in the lives of others."

The three habits that are essential to the contemplative life, says the author, are reading Scripture, thinking, and prayer. "I want you to understand clearly that . . . reading or hearing the word of God must precede pondering it and without time given to serious reflection there will be no genuine prayer."

The contemplative, insists *The Cloud of Unknowing*, is not struggling to get from one place to another, even spiritually, for "love and desire constitute the life of the spirit . . . . We need not strain our spirit in all directions to reach heaven, for we dwell there already through love and desire."

The author of *The Cloud of Unknowing* has no mercy on phony piety. No one can say he had no sense of humor. "The spiritual and physical comportment of those involved in any sort of pseudo-contemplation is apt to appear very eccentric," says he, "whereas God's friends always bear themselves with simple grace. Anyone noticing these deluded folk at prayer might see strange things indeed! If their eyes are open, they are apt to be staring blankly like a madman or peering like one who saw the devil, and well they might, for he is not far off. Sometimes their eyes look like the eyes of wounded sheep near death. Some will let their heads droop to one side, as if a worm were in their ears . . . . They are usually hypocrites."

The Cloud of Unknowing is sometimes cited to support anti-intellectualism. The author does criticize those who "fall victim to their pride, intellectual curiosity, and scholarly knowledge when they reject the common doctrine and guidance of the Church." But the point is *not* that intellectual pursuits are contrary to the contemplative life. Rather, they can be a problem for people who reject church teachings and traditions.

The Cloud takes the individual person quite seriously. Some people will "reach contemplation" with relative ease; for others a long and painful struggle will be necessary. Some people will learn to go about their ordinary daily activities in a contemplative spirit.

The prayer that ends *The Cloud of Unknowing* reveals clearly the anonymous author's intentions: "My dear friend, I bid you farewell now with God's blessing and mine. May God give you and all who love him true peace, wise counsel, and his own interior joy in the fullness of grace. Amen."

Contemporary Application

The author of *The Cloud of Unknowing* insists that in a contemplative life there must be time for reading Scripture, thinking, and prayer. Today he might say that these three elements are essential to any Christian life, not just for those called to monastic contemplation.

To make daily time to read Scripture, and to take the trouble to learn enough about Scripture to read it as it is meant to be read, not with a naive fundamentalist spirit, is nothing short of a radical move. To allow oneself to be challenged, as well as comforted, each day by Scripture, is to open oneself up to becoming no one's person but Christ's, no one's servant but one's neighbor's.

To make time daily to think. Now there's a novel idea. Thomas Edison once said that most people would rather die than think. To think requires opening oneself to ideas, which requires more reading. To keep a journal can be helpful.

To pray each day is the culmination of reading Scripture and thinking. The two come together in a communion with the Spirit present in oneself and in one's life.

Of course, the usual objection is lack of time. Applesauce. We make time for that which we truly value. If we believe that reading Scripture, thinking, and prayer are essential to life, we'll make a few minutes for each, each day.

5
The Writings Of
St. Francis & St. Claire

Quiz time! Who wrote the prayer which begins, "Lord, make me an instrument of your peace"?

St. Francis of Assisi. Right?

Wrong. In his Preface to *Francis and Clare: The Complete Works*, Franciscan Minister General Father John Vaughn writes that the famous prayer for peace has been ascribed to St. Francis only in the last forty years. "Earlier," writes Father Vaughn "—in a small Italian prayerbook, the first known printing—it is ascribed to William the Norman! In addition, the Capuchin Willibrord van Dyke is said to have found it on a holy card ascribed to William the Conqueror!"

Franciscan Fathers Regis J. Armstrong and Ignatius C. Brady, translators of *Francis and Clare*, add that this prayer "can only be found in twentieth-century sources and erroneously attributed to St. Francis." So it goes.

Not to be dejected, however, because there are plenty of authentic writings from St. Francis. The Poverello's writings include

admonitions, short blessings, lengthy prayers, two versions of his
Rule for members of the Franciscan order, letters, and a Rule for
hermitages. The Francis who emerges from his own writings is,
however, quite different from the plaster Francis who stands in
backyard birdbaths all over the country.

Writings by St. Clare, whose story is so closely associated with that
of St. Francis, also have survived.

Probably the most celebrated authentic writing of St. Francis is
"The Canticle of Brother Sun," a beautiful hymn to the created
order which was actually written in three stages. The first and
longest section—written after Francis received the stigmata on
Mount La Verna, in 1224—begins: "Most High, all-powerful, good
Lord, / Yours are the praises, the glory, the honor, and all blessing.
/ To You alone, Most High, do they belong, / and no man is worthy
to mention Your name. / Praised be You, my Lord, with all your crea-
tures, / especially Sir Brother Sun, / Who is the day and through
whom You give us light. / And he is beautiful and radiant with great
splendor; / and bears a likeness of You, Most High One."

Francis praises Sister Moon, the stars, Brother Wind, "and every
kind of weather," Sister Water, Brother Fire, and "our Sister Mother
Earth."

The second, very short, section—written soon after the first as
an attempt to unite the quarreling civil and religious authorities of
Assisi—praises the "Lord, through those who give pardon for Your
Love," those who suffer, and those who "endure in peace."

The final section, also brief, was dictated by the saint on his
deathbed, and includes these words: "Praised be You, my Lord,
through our Sister Bodily Death, / from whom no living man can
escape."

Less well-known, but of great historical value, are St. Francis'
"Admonitions." These twenty-eight brief teachings have been called
"The Franciscan Sermon on the Mount." "It is difficult to deter-

mine the circumstances and dates of their composition," write Fathers Armstrong and Brady, "but it is likely that they were delivered at the gatherings or chapters of the primitive fraternity in which St. Francis was accustomed to deliver spiritual exhortations or admonitions."

The "Admonitions" provide an excellent illustration of the way in which Francis was fond of using Scripture, in which he was clearly steeped on a daily basis, so obvious is his thorough knowledge of it.

Admonition IV, "Let No One Appropriate to Himself the Role of Being Over Others," is a good example: "*I did not come to be served but to serve*, says the Lord. Those who are placed over others should glory in such an office only as much as they would were they assigned the task of washing the feet of the brothers."

Admonition XV, "Poverty of Spirit," squelches romantic interpretations of Francis' love for Lady Poverty: "*Blessed are the poor in spirit for the kingdom of heaven is theirs.* There are many who, applying themselves insistently to prayers and good deeds, engage in much abstinence and many mortifications of their bodies, but they are scandalized and quickly roused to anger by a single word which seems injurious to their person, or by some other things which might be taken from them. These [persons] are not poor in spirit because a person who is truly poor in spirit hates himself (Lk. 14:26) and loves those who strike him on the cheek (Mt. 5:39)."

The "Admonitions" include blessings for "the person who bears with his neighbor in his weakness to the degree that he would wish to be sustained by him if he were in a similar situation."

Only two documents survive direct from the hand of St. Francis. One is the Letter to Brother Leo, "preserved on a small piece of parchment," write Fathers Armstrong and Brady, "that Brother Leo, a close companion of St. Francis during his last years, treasured." The other is a parchment on which St. Francis wrote some Praises and Blessings for Brother Leo.

The "Letter to Brother Leo"—almost painfully brief—is the embodiment of what modern psychologists call "nondirective counseling." It also highlights the friendship of Francis and Leo. After asking Brother Leo to wish "your Brother Francis health and peace!" Francis continues:

"I speak to you, my son, as a mother .... In whatever way it seems best to you to please the Lord God, and to follow His footprints and His poverty, do this with the blessing of God and my obedience. And if you believe it necessary for the well-being of your soul, or to find comfort, and you wish to come to me, Leo, come!"

St. Francis was not above calling priests to task. In "A Letter to the Clergy," Francis urges priests to keep their churches clean, and to give equal importance to the Eucharist and to the Scriptures: "... [the Body and Blood of the Lord] is left by many in dirty places, carried about in a miserable manner .... Even His sacred written words are sometimes left to be trampled underfoot .... Well then, let us quickly and firmly amend our ways ..."

Anticipating the Vatican II era by hundreds of years, Francis writes late in life, in his "Letter to the Entire Order," that Masses said by a priest in private are inappropriate (and he seems to know nothing of the idea of concelebration):

"Therefore I admonish and urge in the Lord that only one Mass ... be celebrated each day in the places in which the brothers stay. If, however, there should be more than one priest in that place, let one be content, for the sake of charity, to assist at the celebration of the other priest ..."

A Eucharistic hymn which appears in the same letter emphasizes the divine humility: "O sublime humility! / O humble sublimity! / That the Lord of the Universe, God and the Son of God, / so humbles Himself / that for our salvation / He hides Himself under the little form of bread! / Look, brothers, at the humility of God / and *pour out your hearts before Him* [Ps. 61:9]!"

The origins of St. Clare's relationship with St. Francis are lost in the mists of legend, but we do know that on the evening of March 19, 1212, Francis received her commitment to follow Christ in the Franciscan way. Joined by other women, Clare lived in an enclosed convent at San Damiano until her death in 1253, and is honored as the foundress of the Poor Clares.

Remarkably, it seems that Clare was the one who clung to the Franciscan ideal of poverty. "While the friars were accepting papal indults that relaxed their practice of poverty," say Fathers Armstrong and Brady, "Clare was courageously clinging to the primitive ideals and challenging the Holy See to allow her and her sisters to maintain the charism of poverty, which she had received from Francis himself . . . . Thus the expression of Franciscan life depicted in the Rule of St. Clare is more demanding in many respects than the life of the Friars Minor."

St. Clare seems, however, to have written much less than St. Francis. Five letters from Clare, and her Rule, are the only clearly authentic documents. "The Testament of St. Clare," and "The Blessing Attributed to St. Clare," are included in the *Francis and Clare* volume, but it is doubtful that they were actually authored by Clare.

The four Letters of Clare to Blessed Agnes of Prague deal with various aspects of Franciscan spirituality—heavily conditioned by the romanticism of the 13th century. Clare describes Christ in these terms: "Whose power is stronger, / Whose generosity is more abundant, / Whose appearance is more beautiful, / Whose love is more tender, / Whose courtesy is more gracious."

St. Clare's Rule, as noted above, preserves a serious dedication to evangelical poverty: "[The sisters] are not to receive or hold onto any possessions or property [acquired] through an intermediary, or even anything that might reasonably be called property, except as much land as necessity requires for the integrity and the proper seclusion of the monastery; and this land is not to be cultivated except as a garden for the needs of the sisters."

It was Francis, however (in "The Canticle of Brother Sun") who summarized the spirit embraced by both the friars and the Poor Ladies of St. Clare: "Praise and bless my Lord and give Him thanks / and serve Him with great humility."

Contemporary Application

One of the problems with being a saint, as Dorothy Day once remarked, is that when people think you're a saint they can put you on a pedestal and no longer take you seriously. How seriously do we take Francis' dedication to the spirit of "Lady Poverty"?

Those who live in the affluent post-industrial-age western nations often relativize Francis' message to the point of fictionalizing it. In fact, Francis insisted that simplicity of life is essential to a Christian existence.

The dominant culture is one with the philosophy of materialism. The trouble with materialism is that it divides people from one another, it does not encourage sharing. If I have a brand new car and you don't, that car almost inevitably comes between us. It stimulates resentment. If I live in a beautiful house, but you live in a modest, unimpressive house, my house comes between us. If I have lots of fashionable clothes, but you don't, to one degree or another my clothes prevent our coming together fully as friends.

There are no easy answers as to how particular Christians should embody the Christian imperative toward spiritual poverty and a simple lifestyle. This is a principle, as Francis knew, however, that must have tangible consequences in any Christian's life, if faith is to be authentic.

6
Dante Alighieri's
The Divine Comedy

Dante Alighieri was born in Florence, Italy, in 1265. His family, says James Collins, in *Pilgrim in Love: An Introduction to Dante and His Spirituality*, was what "we might describe as 'upper middle class' . . . . He was baptized at Easter in the beautiful baptistry of St. John (*bel San Giovanni*, he called it) which still stands in all its splendor facing the Cathedral of Florence."

Dante's parents died when he was still a child, and the poet recorded only one event from his youth—his meeting with Beatrice when they were both nine years old, an encounter which he described as "love at first sight." Some scholars deny that Beatrice was an actual historical person, notes Collins, but "most commentators agree that she was nine-year-old Beatrice Portinari," from a family which lived near the Alighieri household.

Beatrice died in her early twenties, which was a terrible blow to Dante. Later, Beatrice became a central figure in the *Divine Comedy*, her role, remarks Collins, that of "a sacrament of God's creative love" for Dante.

Dante loved Florence, the city of his birth, and in 1296 was elected to the "council of a hundred men," a sort of city council. Four years later, accused—unjustly—of political corruption and opposition to the pope, Dante was permanently exiled from his beloved Florence, sentenced to death by burning should he ever return.

For the next twenty-one years, Dante wandered Italy, dependent on wealthy patrons of the arts for hospitality and financial support. His last years were spent, explains James Collins, "in Ravenna as a guest of Guido da Polenta," where he worked on his *Comedy*, finishing it shortly before his death from malarial fever, September 14, 1321, at the age of fifty-six.

The *Divine Comedy* is a three-volume poem, "certainly the greatest single poem ever penned by man," comments Dante translator John Ciardi. In the first volume, the *Inferno* (*Hell*), Dante describes his journey to the depths of evil. The next volume, *Purgatorio* (*Purgatory*) is the poet's account of his journey to the renunciation of sin, the purifying journey upwards toward God. Volume 3, the *Paradiso* (*Paradise*), brings Dante to an experience of cosmic ecstasy where he hears "the laughter of the universe."

It is important to know, writes James Collins, that Dante's basic purpose is to present an allegorical tale, "to describe the states of the human soul . . . . Hell, then, is an allegory of the soul caught in the sin it has willingly chosen. Purgatory pictures the soul's struggle to be free of the bonds of sin, to become beautiful and whole again in the image of God, as it was created. Paradise is the image of the soul's foretaste even in this life of the joy and ecstasy which union with God gives." Dante models his masterpiece on the epic poems of classical literature.

"Halfway along the journey of our life," begins Dante, in the *Inferno*, "/ Having strayed from the right path and lost it, / I awoke to find myself in a dark wood." The allegory begins with images of confusion and anguish, of a meaningless existence. "The restless heart of the Christian pilgrim," says Collins, "is . . . the main prerequisite for making the journey with Dante."

The words over the gates of Hell summarize the meaning of this first book. "Through me," reads the inscription, "is the way into the suffering city; / through me the way into eternal pain; / through me the way among the lost people; / . . . . abandon all hope, you who enter." Dante's guide, the "pagan" poet Virgil, comments: "We have come to the place where I told you / that you would see the miserable people / who have lost the good of the intellect [that is, the human soul]." The point, remarks commentator Francis Fergusson, is to present the human person "as totally lost."

Dante's journey through Hell consists of a downward spiral through several circles of evil. The least serious sins are seen in the beginning and gradually an increasing wickedness is portrayed in the succeeding circles.

Thus, sexual sins are portrayed as the most natural, the easiest to commit, and the least harmful. Next come sins of violence and fraud. And the very worst sin of all, at the bottom circle of Hell, is treachery, the betrayal of trust and human relationships.

Note that Dante did not invent this hierarchy of sins. He found it in the writings of Aristotle, St. Augustine and St. Thomas Aquinas.

The spirits in Hell blame God for their fate, they accuse their parents and the whole human race. The wages of sin (to paraphrase St. Paul) are alienation and isolation from human community.

The *Purgatorio* (". . . that second kingdom / wherein the human spirit is made clean, / becoming worthy to ascend to heaven.") tells of Dante's journey of enlightenment, change, and conversion. Still guided by Virgil, the poet climbs Purgatory's "seven storey mountain," (from which Thomas Merton took the title of his famous autobiography).

The terraces of Purgatory reflect allegorically the soul's process of conversion, including repentance of the seven capital sins—pride, envy, anger, sloth, avarice, gluttony, and lust—forms of love gone awry. Dante then enters an earthly paradise where, among other events, he is reminded that, "The Scriptures, the creeds and the sacraments of the Church—all true reflections from God—are nonetheless only pale reflections of God."

One of the most powerful messages of the *Purgatorio* is Dante's deeply Catholic conviction of the basic goodness of human nature. "He strongly affirmed the truth," insists James Collins, "that we are images of God, that deep down within all of us is an untarnished beauty: the human heart, innocent, loving, capable of good acts of authentic love."

Of the three parts of the *Divine Comedy*, the *Paradiso* is often the most difficult for modern readers to grasp. "We readers in the twentieth century," writes Collins, "must do our 'homework' in order to understand the idiom and ideas of medieval theology and mysticism [in the *Divine Comedy*]."

Among the dominant images of *Paradise* are those of music and light. Dante writes of a joy beyond description, a joy totally beyond any joy this life can offer.

Dante encounters individual people in Paradise, but their earthly appearance has been changed into various kinds of light. "They continue to speak, act, sing, and dance," notes Collins, "but their personalities glow and sparkle with the intense warmth and light of love." St. Peter, for example, "glows red with indignation and anger, as he denounces the corrupt behavior of Pope Boniface VIII and other popes who are neglecting their pastoral care of the Church on earth."

Dante's guide in Paradise is Beatrice, the young woman he loved on earth. Centuries before space travel, Beatrice leads Dante effortlessly from one planet to another where, among others, he meets St. Thomas Aquinas, St. Francis, St. Dominic, St. Bonaventure, and Mary, whom Dante calls "Lady of Heaven."

Beatrice, the angels and the saints, sing together, "Holy, Holy, Holy," in praise of the Triune God. "What I saw," writes Dante, "seemed to me the smile of the universe . . . Oh joy! Oh unspeakable gladness! Oh life completed by love and peace!"

Dante and Beatrice enter, says James Collins, "the last heaven, the Empyrean, the heaven of pure light beyond time and space." Dante gazes on the heavenly kingdom, "which has the form of a pure white rose of countless petals."

The end of Dante's journey is to see humanity at one with God. But the poet's final words are spoken from earth, gazing up at the universe. He identifies himself with humanity, all who are still on their earthly pilgrimage. And his message is clear: how good and trustworthy is "the Love that moves the sun and the other stars."

Contemporary Application

Dante's allegorical fantasy poem lends itself to understanding our own experience at any given time, no matter what shape our lives may be in, no matter how we may feel at a particular moment.

Human experience is not neat and well-ordered, however. We do not progress step by step from sin toward virtue, from the "hell" of our own mistakes, foolishness, self-hatred, and plain meanness toward the heaven of a life at complete peace with God and neighbor. Rather, we bounce around.

Dante is clear about his belief in human freedom. People wind up in his *Inferno* only because they chose to be there. Still, his central message is one of hope. He proclaims a God who loves, a universe which is ultimately benevolent, a firm belief in the certainty of forgiveness and salvation. His image of a universe that is laughing with joy is one that fits the space age perfectly. The universe astronauts go sailing in is a reflection of its joyful Creator.

The *Purgatorio* is an image for much of life. In it Dante portrays his own experience of alienation from Florence, the city he loves, and in so doing he describes the universal human experience of being on pilgrimage toward the eternal kingdom. Hope! he cries. Hope, even when the night is darkest, for your hope will not be disappointed!

7
The Way Of A Pilgrim

The Way of a Pilgrim is an Eastern Orthodox spiritual classic that is treasured by many modern teachers of prayer. Penned in mid-19th century Russia, it was first published in 1884 after the manuscript was discovered by a Russian monk visiting the famous monastic island of Mount Athos, in Greece. The book appeared in English in 1930, although it doesn't seem to have had much exposure in the U.S. until the 1960s when many learned about it from the popular J. D. Salinger novel, *Franny and Zooey*. Translated literally from Russian, the actual title is, *Candid Narratives of a Pilgrim to His Spiritual Father*.

The anonymous author reveals little about himself or his past apart from saying that as a child, apparently through some accident, he had lost the use of his left arm. *The Way of a Pilgrim* otherwise confines itself to the story of how the author became a pilgrim, walking the Russian countryside in prayer, reflection, and conversation with others. The central theme of the book is the Pilgrim's discovery of and love for the Prayer of Jesus.

The Way of a Pilgrim begins with great charm and simplicity. "By the grace of God," writes the Pilgrim, "I am a Christian man, by my actions a great sinner, and by calling a homeless wanderer of the humblest birth who roams from place to place. My worldly goods are a knapsack with some dried bread in it on my back, and in my breast-pocket a Bible. And that is all."

The author then explains how he became a pilgrim. "On the 24th Sunday after Pentecost," he writes, "I went to church to say my prayers there during the Liturgy. The First Epistle of St. Paul to the Thessalonians was being read, and among other words I heard these—'Pray without ceasing.' It was this text, more than any other, which forced itself upon my mind, and I began to think how it was possible to pray without ceasing, since a man has to concern himself with other things also in order to make a living."

In his own Bible the pious Russian locates the words he heard in church, and sure enough he was not mistaken. ". . . we ought always, at all times and in all places, to pray with uplifted hands."

He is extremely puzzled. " 'What ought I to do?' I thought. 'Where shall I find someone to explain it to me?' " Innocent of modern historical methods of biblical interpretation, he takes St. Paul's words at face value and begins the quest for a solution to his problem—he becomes a pilgrim (almost a social class unto itself in 19th-century Russia).

First the Pilgrim journeys to many churches where he hears countless fine sermons on prayer. But none tells him how to "pray without ceasing." So he resolves "by God's help to look for some experienced and skilled person who would give me in conversation that teaching about unceasing prayer which drew me so urgently."

Wandering Russia, reading his Bible always, the Pilgrim inquires at every opportunity about a spiritual teacher who may be able to help him. For over a year he travels, now and then meeting a wise spiritual man, but finding no satisfactory answer to his question. With infinite patience he reports sadly of one teacher after another,

"He did not explain the matter," or "He did not give me the explanation."

Finally, however, the Pilgrim's persistence is rewarded. One evening as he walks along he is "overtaken by an old man who looked like a cleric of some sort," who turns out to be a monk from a nearby monastery. The monk invites the Pilgrim to come with him for food and a good night's rest. "I did not feel like going," remarks the Pilgrim, somewhat impatiently. He informs the monk that he is not looking for a place to sleep and in his knapsack he has plenty of dried bread to eat.

The monk asks the Pilgrim what he really wants, the Pilgrim tells his story, and the monk responds: "Thank God, my dear brother, for having revealed to you this unappeasable desire for unceasing interior prayer. Recognize in it the call of God, and calm yourself."

So the Pilgrim and the monk walk to the monastery, the latter all the while delivering himself of a homily on prayer, the Pilgrim speaking not a word. "The Christian," says the monk, "is bound to perform many good works, but before all else what he ought to do is to pray, for without prayer no other good work whatever can be accomplished."

The Pilgrim is patient, but also he wants to lose no time. "During this talk," he remarks, "we had almost reached the monastery. And so as not to lose touch with this wise old man, and to get what I wanted more quickly, I hastened to say, 'Be so kind, Reverend Father, as to show me what prayer without ceasing means and how it is learnt. I see you know all about these things.' "

The two enter the monk's cell, and the Pilgrim finally learns the answer to his question. " 'The continuous interior Prayer of Jesus,' instructs the monk, 'is a constant uninterrupted calling upon the divine Name of Jesus with the lips, in the spirit, in the heart; while forming a mental picture of His constant presence, and imploring His grace, during every occupation, at all times, in all places, even during sleep. The appeal is couched in these terms, "Lord Jesus

Christ, have mercy on me." One who accustoms himself to this appeal experiences as a result so deep a consolation and so great a need to offer the prayer always, that he can no longer live without it, and it will continue to voice itself within him of its own accord.' "

The Pilgrim is overjoyed, and begs the monk to teach him "how to gain the habit" of the Prayer of Jesus. The monk shows the Pilgrim a book called *The Philokalia* (in Russian, *Dobrotolyubie*, which means *The Love of Spiritual Beauty*), a famous collection of spiritual writings from eleven centuries by Fathers of the Eastern Orthodox Church. "Read this book," the monk instructs the Pilgrim, ". . . it contains the full and detailed science of constant interior prayer, set forth by twenty-five holy Fathers . . . . As the revered Nicephorus said, 'It leads one to salvation without labor and sweat.' "

After further instruction based on teachings in *The Philokalia*, the monk sends the Pilgrim on his way, cautioning him to "always come back to him and tell him everything, making a very frank confession and report; for the inward process could not go on properly and successfully without the guidance of a teacher."

A peasant hires the Pilgrim for the summer to look after his garden, and gives him "a little thatched hut" to live in. At first the Pilgrim finds joy in saying the Prayer, but soon becomes "lazy and bored and overwhelmingly sleepy." Visits with the monk—now his *starets* or spiritual father—enable the Pilgrim to cope with difficulties in saying the Prayer of Jesus.

At summer's end, the Pilgrim is saddened by the death of his *starets*. "Weeping freely I bade him farewell, and thanked him for the fatherly teaching he had given my wretched self, and as a blessing and a keepsake I begged for the rosary with which he said his prayers."

Released from his garden duties by the arrival of autumn, the Pilgrim takes the wages he earned, two roubles, locates "a worn and old copy of *The Philokalia*", priced at two roubles, and buys it. "I was delighted with it. I mended my book as much as I could, I made a cover for it with a piece of cloth, and put it into my breast pocket with my Bible."

The Pilgrim reports that after wandering about "for a long time in different districts, having for my fellow traveller the Prayer of Jesus," after many futile attempts to find work (no one wants to hire a man with the use of but one arm), and after much study of *The Philokalia*, one day the Prayer deepens.

"I had the feeling," the Pilgrim writes, "that the Prayer had, so to speak, by its own action passed from my lips to my heart. That is to say, it seemed as though my heart in its ordinary beating began to say the words of the Prayer within at each beat . . . . I gave up saying the Prayer with my lips. I simply listened carefully to what my heart was saying."

Many adventures lie ahead for the Pilgrim, but his basic message remains the same, and it's as valid today as when it was first written down: ". . . prayer is the chief and strongest means for our renewal and well-being."

Contemporary Application

Is it practical to think of using the Jesus prayer in today's busy world? It is, provided one keeps in mind that he or she is not living in the quiet Russian countryside that the Pilgrim took for granted. It's important, too, to take into account individual temperament and unique personal rhythms. Keep in mind that unlike the good Pilgrim we cannot assume that because St. Paul instructed his readers to "pray always," that what he meant was what we may think he meant.

There are people today who claim to have experienced the "deepening" of the Jesus prayer—its automatic repetition within themselves—that the Pilgrim described. It is, then, evidently possible for this to happen. There are people, however, for whom such a goal would be frustrating, perhaps even harmful.

Many find a more helpful approach is to use the Jesus prayer during times of private prayer. One woman prays the rosary in the traditional fashion while taking her daily walk, then once the rosary is over she switches to the Jesus prayer for the rest of her walk.

A man in his mid-40's uses the Jesus prayer as a way to center himself during his morning prayer time, before his wife and children are awake. After fifteen minutes of Scripture reading, he spends fifteen minutes silently repeating the Jesus prayer.

8
St. Therese Of Lisieux:
The Story Of A Soul

St. Therese of Lisieux (1873-1897) had an intense dislike for praying the rosary. She said that, "the recitation of the rosary is more difficult for me than the wearing of an instrument of penance." She also believed that to allow herself sometimes to fall asleep during meditation was an act of faith. What kind of saint is this?

The Story of a Soul, by the young French Carmelite nun whose full religious name was Sister Therese of the Child Jesus and of the Holy Face, ranks among the most popular of the modern spiritual classics. Like any classic, however, it must be read as what it is: in this case, the work of a 19th-century French, Carmelite nun, from an economically comfortable background. Each of these factors is important. Each must be taken seriously if the reader would grasp the truth St. Therese embodied rather than some romantic religious chimera.

The Story of a Soul is actually three manuscripts. The first (Chapters 1 through 8) was written for Therese's older sister Pauline

(Mother Agnes), who was Prioress of the Carmelite community at Lisieux from 1893-1896. In this manuscript Therese discusses her childhood from her earliest memories until her long-awaited acceptance into the Carmelite order at the age of fifteen. Therese praises her mother and father, and describes the warmth of her relationships with her sisters. She remarks on "how quickly those sunny years passed by, those years of my childhood, but what a sweet imprint they have left on my soul!"

The second manuscript (Chapter 9) is the shortest of the three. Therese wrote it for her sister, Marie (Sister Marie of the Sacred Heart). The translator, Carmelite Father John Clarke, calls this concise document, "the jewel of all Therese's writings." Here Therese displays faultless perception as she reveals her discovery of the very heart of the Christian life: "I understand so well that it is only love which makes us acceptable to God . . ."

Therese does not hesitate to claim for herself the vocations of warrior, priest, apostle, doctor, and martyr. "I feel in me the vocation of PRIEST," she writes; and yet, "I admire and envy the humility of St. Francis of Assisi and I feel the *vocation* of imitating him in refusing . . . the Priesthood."

Although Therese surely had great respect for the Church's teaching that only men may receive Holy Orders, she makes no reference to her ineligibility for ordination due to being female. Instead, she follows St. Francis in "refusing" the priesthood.

The climax of this short section comes when Therese recounts her discovery of her vocation: ". . . my vocation, at last I have found it . . . MY VOCATION IS LOVE!"

The final manuscript (Chapters 10 and 11) was written for Mother Marie de Gonzague, then Prioress, by Therese during her last illness. Here Therese discusses her short seven years in religious life. "There is much in these concluding chapters," writes Father Clarke, "that reveal the real Therese."

Therese acknowledges an intense crisis of faith. It is as if she must
believe in spite of her unbelief. ". . . while I do not have *the joy of
faith*, I am trying to carry out its works at least." Faith becomes for
Therese not like a veil, but like "a wall which reaches right up to
the heavens and covers the starry firmament." Yet she thrills at
being in the same convent with her own sisters: "How can anyone
say it is more perfect to separate oneself from one's blood relatives?
. . . I am happy to combat *as a family* for the glory of heaven's King."

"I understand now," Therese writes, articulating a principle of
the spiritual life as valid in the homes of ordinary people as in a
Carmelite convent, "that charity consists in bearing with the faults
of others, in not being surprised at their weakness, in being edified
by the smallest acts of virtue we see them practice."

Later, Therese shows herself a true disciple of St. Paul: "The most
beautiful thoughts are nothing without good works." She discusses
her method of prayer: ". . . I say very simply to God what I wish to
say, without composing beautiful sentences, and He always understands me."

It may be that *Story of a Soul* proves the old adage, "Any translation is a betrayal." Even the title sounds better in the original
French: *Histoire d'une Ame*. To scan the book in Therese's French,
as she actually wrote it, is to escape some of what Father Clarke
calls "the sweet sentimentality which none of us appreciates."
"Springtime Story of a Little White Flower," Therese's title for the
first manuscript, sounds less cloying in her own words: "*Histoire
printaniere d'une petite Fleur blanche*."

The spirit of 19th-century bourgeois French Catholic piety fills
the book. Yet in spite of that fact, what is most remarkable is the
way the patient reader is able to follow Therese's progress in the
spiritual life. It would not be unfair to say that Therese grew from
a crybaby into a courageous, faith-filled woman—indeed, into a
saint. Yet the modern reader does need to be patient with the
"sweet sentimentality" that escapes hardly a page of Therese's

book, and dig for the prophetic witness she gave to the rock-hard truths of the Christian life.

Early in the book the reader may be struck with how frequently Therese quotes directly from, or refers to Scripture. A quick count reveals 155 Biblical references in the less than 250 pages of the English text. Therese must have steeped herself in Scripture, to be able to draw these Bible references and quotations from thin air while writing—even later when she was so seriously ill with tuberculosis. Intended or not, St. Therese of Lisieux sends a challenge to modern Catholics to spend more time with Scripture.

Indeed, as Father Clarke points out, St. Therese bases her famous "little way" (a spirituality of doing the small things in life with heroic faith) on three texts from the Old Testament: "Whoever is a little one, let him come to me" (Proverbs 9:4); "For to him that is little, mercy will be shown" (Wisdom 6:7); "As one whom a mother caresses, so will I comfort you; you shall be carried at the breasts, and upon the knees they shall fondle you" (Isaiah 66:12-13).

Another remarkable characteristic of Therese's spirituality reflected in *Story of a Soul*, is the author's evident love for nature. Therese sometimes sounds like a Franciscan nature mystic. Referring to her early childhood, she writes: "Already I was in love with the *wide-open spaces*. Space and the gigantic fir trees, the branches sweeping down to the ground, left in my heart an impression similar to the one I experience still today at the sight of nature."

Here is how Therese formulates the truth that God's love for each person is endless and unconditional: "Just as the sun shines simultaneously on the tall cedars and on each little flower as though it were alone on the earth, so Our Lord is occupied particularly with each soul as though there were no others like it. And just as in nature all the seasons are arranged in such a way as to make the humblest daisy bloom on a set day, in the same way, everything works out for the good of each soul."

Parents can take a lesson on raising children from *Story of a Soul*. Therese remarks time after time, in the first manuscript, on how as a young child she was surrounded with the love of her family: "God was pleased all through my life to surround me with *love*, and the first memories I have are stamped with smiles and the most tender caresses." Many religious educators of the 1980s would suggest that Therese received her faith in a loving God in the most effective way possible, through the love of her parents and older sisters.

Perhaps as the baby of the family it is predictable that Therese would receive much affection. Yet Therese remarks on the practical forms love took when, after her mother's death, when she was four years old, her oldest sister Pauline took over: "I wonder at times how you were able to raise me with so much *love* and tenderness without spoiling me, for it's true you never allowed an imperfection to pass, you never scolded me without reason, and you *never* went back on something once you made a decision." Many of today's experts would applaud Pauline's parenting skills.

This first part of Therese's book is not without humor. She tells a story of playing with dolls: "To console me once she [her older sister Celine] took one of her dolls and said: 'My dear, embrace your Aunt!' The doll was in such a rush to embrace me tenderly that her two little arms went up *my nose*. Celine, who hadn't done it purposely, looked at me stupefied; the doll was dangling from my nose."

Therese's decision to think of herself as "a little flower" has been romanticized over the years to the point that her actual reason for choosing such an image is easily overlooked. Therese used the image of a "little flower" to convey the idea of strength in weakness, much as did St. Paul when he wrote: "I am content with weaknesses, insults, hardships, persecutions, and difficulties for Christ's sake. For when I am weak, then I am strong" (2 Cor. 12:10). Therese had nothing foolish in mind when she called herself "a little flower."

The final words of *Story of a Soul* sum up Therese's life and message. Writing with great effort only days before her death, in a last incomplete sentence, Therese says that, "I go to Him with confidence and love . . ."

This is the spirituality of St. Therese of Lisieux in a nutshell: to live one's ordinary life to the fullest "with confidence and love," and to face death not with fear, but "with confidence and love."

Contemporary Application

The autobiography of St. Therese of Lisieux stands in a direct line that began with St. Augustine's *Confessions*, with Thomas Merton's *The Seven Storey Mountain* the best-known 20th century example. In her life story she reflects on how God was at work in the events of her life, from her earliest days. Listen to your life, she might as well have said, see it for the mystery that it is, and recognize God there.

Therese was ahead of her time in several ways. She recognized that her vocation, regardless of the incidentals of her life, was "to love." Able to distinguish between the essentials and the non-essentials of the Christian life, she insisted on the value of reaching out to others with a love communicated through prayer.

Her life was obscure in the extreme, yet by the writing of a single book Therese showed the world that heroism can best be measured only in relation to the circumstances of the individual life. The hidden life of Therese of Lisieux can do the world as much good as the highly public life of a Mother Teresa of Calcutta.

Though its messages are many, perhaps the bottom line for making sense of *Story of a Soul* today is its witness to the value of prayer. Prayer, says St. Therese of Lisieux, is vital to any Christian life, no matter how busy.

9
Caryll Houselander's
The Reed Of God

English artist and writer Caryll Houselander (1901-1954) was, in several ways, a psychological and spiritual mirror of her anxious century. Caryll's parents divorced when she was a child, and it took years for her to overcome the emotional consequences of this experience.

She also, as they say, smoked like a chimney. "She smoked as she worked," wrote Maisie Ward in her biography, *Caryll Houselander: That Divine Eccentric,* "she smoked from morning to night, she woke in the night and smoked." Then one day, quite suddenly, she abandoned cigarettes never to smoke again.

Houselander was in the habit of covering her face with some sort of white powder. Upon first meeting her, people thought her an odd duck, indeed. "My husband had prepared me for Caryll's appearance . . ." wrote Maisie Ward. "Yet as I stood waiting outside the door of her flat and she came up behind me laden with parcels I was conscious of a genuine shock. The dead-white face, the thick glasses, the fringe of red hair, a touch somehow of the grotesque—it was so surprising as to take one's breath away."

A few minutes in Caryll Houselander's presence, however, seems to have been enough to make virtually anyone her friend. "But we had hardly exchanged a word," adds Maisie Ward, "when we felt (both of us, I could swear) the perfect ease of long intimacy, and began a conversation to be picked up at any moment thereafter."

Caryll Houselander was a sculptor of wood. She produced hundreds of beautiful figures, some of which grace English Catholic churches to this day. ". . . there is no work on earth," she confided to a friend, "which in my mind is more soothing and healing than carving wood."

She had a special gift, too, for helping those with emotional and psychological problems. She claimed that having been psychologically broken in her youth, she was able to help others with similar difficulties. Professional therapists sent patients to Caryll for help. Often she could "bring a person round" when the doctor could not.

"If there were more good listeners," she said, "there would not be nearly so many neurotics." She often remarked that she understood neurotics not only because she had once been one, but because she still was one. The neurotic, too, can be a saint, she said. "The one essential for sanctity is the capacity to love."

Caryll Houselander was ahead of her time regarding today's popular wedding of psychological insights with theology. To a young woman she tried to help through frequent spells of depression, she wrote: "I agree with you indeed about the 'importance of living.' I go further: it seems to me that the very great thing is to be able to *enjoy* life."

Her social conscience was finely tuned. She was among the first after World War II to suggest that Christians "make public (and of course secret) reparation" for the atom bomb holocausts at Hiroshima and Nagasaki.

Caryll Houselander died of cancer, October 12, 1954.

Houselander wrote several books and many magazine articles, but *The Reed of God* teeters on the edge of becoming a modern classic. Maisie Ward called this book an "unremitting attack on unreality in life and in religion—the unreality that worships Christ in church but refuses to see Him in mankind, the unreality that takes refuge in organizations and committees, thinks of humanity instead of men, and fondly dreams that sociology and reformed economic conditions can take the place of religion."

Originally published in England in 1944, Houselander calls *The Reed of God* a "contemplation." Although whole chapters at a time make no mention of her, *The Reed of God* is an extended meditation on the meaning of the Blessed Virgin Mary. "Nothing but things essential *for us,*" she wrote, "are revealed to us about the Mother of God: the fact that she was wed to the Holy Spirit and bore Christ into the world. Our crowning joy is that she did this as a lay person and through the ordinary daily life that we all live."

Still, "a very great many people" still think of Mary as "someone who would never do anything that we do . . . To many she is the Madonna of the Christmas card, immobile, seated forever in the immaculately clean stable of golden straw and shining snow. She is not real; nothing about her is real, not even the stable in which Love was born."

The Reed of God includes its share of a romanticized piety characteristic of Catholicism during the 1940s and '50s. For example, Houselander's remarks about virginity are true, but expressed in a way that today may perplex more often than it enlightens. "Virginity," Houselander wrote, "is really the whole offering of soul and body to be consumed in the fire of love and changed into the flame of its glory."

The remarkable thing about this little book, however, is the extent to which its author managed to sidestep the popular romantic piety of her times. Page after page is filled with concise, hard-hitting insights into the nature of an authentic Christian life. Caryll Houselander's Mariology anticipated Vatican II by twenty years.

"[Our Lady]," she wrote, "is not only human; she is humanity."

"The one thing that she did and does is the one thing that we all have to do, namely, to bear Christ into the world."

The fundamental understanding of spirituality which Caryll Houselander took for granted rings as true today as the day it was written. To wit, at some length:

"There are many people in the world who cultivate a curious state which they call 'the spiritual life.' They often complain that they have very little time to devote to the 'spiritual life.' The only time that they do not regard as wasted is the time they can devote to pious exercises: praying, reading, meditations, and visiting the church.

"All the time spent in earning a living, cleaning the home, caring for the children, making and mending clothes, cooking, and all the other manifold duties and responsibilities, is regarded as wasted.

"Yet it is really through ordinary human life and the things of every hour of every day that union with God comes about."

At the center of this conception of spirituality is a conviction that it's nothing short of amazing to find on any spiritual writer's mind in 1944. Remember, this was written at a time when it was still common in popular piety for the human body, with its senses and sexuality, to be viewed as a constant threat to one's eternal destiny: "It is impossible to say too often or too strongly that human nature, body and soul together, is the material for God's will in us."

Caryll Houselander was absolutely orthodox in her perceptions, even when popular piety was not. This may well be due to the fact that she was on intimate terms with Scripture. Years before it became popular again among Catholics, she insisted that familiarity with Scripture was essential to a Christian life. ". . . it is really necessary, in our search for Christ, to read the Gospel, and to read it all without flinching; or if we must flinch, at least without giving up the attempt."

At the heart of the Gospel, Houselander knew, is a two-part spirituality. She also understood that the two parts may never be separated: love of God and love for other people. "There are those who cannot keep the first commandment [to love God] because in their heart of hearts they are afraid to keep the second [to love other people]."

So seriously did she take the Incarnation that she compared Christ present in the Eucharist to Christ present in everyday people. "That which is true of the Host is true of people," she wrote. "We cannot discern God's presence through our senses, but faith tells us that we should treat one another with the reverence that we give to the Host.

"We need to bring to other people faith like that which we bring to the Blessed Sacrament."

A theologian in every sense of the word except the formal academic one, Caryll Houselander understood the central importance of one's image or concept of God. One's perspective on life in general, one's attitude toward religion and toward relationships with other people—all this and more is directly related to the image of God implied by one's feelings about God. For Caryll Houselander, an essential question for any adult Christian to ask himself or herself is, "What do you mean when you say God?"

"In the degree of the falseness of our conception of God, we restrict and narrow our interests and sympathies; we grow in intolerance and hardness or in a flabbiness which turns to a rot of sweetness like a diabetes of the soul.

"In the degree of the truth of our conception of Him, our minds grow broader, deeper, and warmer; our hearts grow wiser and kinder; our humour deeper and more tender; we become more aware of the wonder of life; our senses become more sensitive; our sympathies stronger; our capacity for giving and for receiving greater; our minds are more radiant with a burning light, and the light is the light of Christ."

Caryll Houselander: artist, oddball, mystic, friend, and, in the end, suffering servant. In the midst of her last illness, she clung to life, loved life with a passion that did not want to die. "I honestly long," she said, "to be told 'a hundred per cent cure' and to return to this life and celebrate it with gramophone records, giggling and gin."

Contemporary Application

Caryll Houselander was one of those writers who can't not write. When she was on a writing jag she would sit on the toilet seat lid in her bathroom, writing where she could have light without disturbing her friend with whom she shared an apartment. She wrote *The Reed of God* this way.

As Maisie Ward remarked, *The Reed of God* is an attack against phoniness in religion. And there's room for rooting out phoniness in almost anyone's religion.

Popular contemporary forms of religious phoniness include the view that anyone who doesn't join the movement I belong to doesn't measure up; the view that unless you pray the way I do you're not really praying; the position that the only real Christian is one who protests the things I protest; the belief that since Vatican II the church is going to hell in a wicker basket; the belief that anything from before the council is worthless; the pious attitude that religion, politics, economics, and lifestyle are unrelated to one another; and the equally pious attitude that you're not a real Christian unless your politics and lifestyle meet my approval. And there are many others.

The reason all of these are phony is that each puts Christianity in a small box with a little brass padlock on it. Each implies a complete and absolute grasp of the mind of God.

10
Butler's Lives Of The Saints

Stories of the saints serve in Catholic spirituality, especially, as a reminder that we are not alone. The saints are heroes, but more than that. They belong to what is traditionally called "the communion of saints." That is, they are present, with us still, somehow involved in the mystery of our lives. When we gather for the Eucharist, we call upon the saints to be with us, and we believe that they are.

Butler's Lives of the Saints is the best-known, most complete collection of stories about saints ever compiled. Each of its four volumes runs to over 700 pages. The late poet Phyllis McGinley, no slouch on saints herself (she wrote something of a modern classic, *Saint Watching*), called *Butler's* "that famous, learned and hortatory set of volumes." You can find virtually any saint, except those canonized in the last few years, in *Butler's*.

Though much of the material about saints from ancient times is largely legendary (and the current edition acknowledges this), *Butler's* still makes inspiring, informative, and entertaining reading for adults and youngsters. The example set by saints ancient and modern still serves as an encouragement to a Christian life in our own times.

The first edition of *Butler's Lives of the Saints* was written by Alban Butler, an English priest and scholar, and appeared between 1756 and 1759. Alban Butler seems to have been dearly loved by those who knew him, and his *Lives* became a best seller. An English lady, Mrs. Paston, who lived near the College of St. Omer, where Butler was president, wrote of him following his death in 1773:

"Dear Mr. Butler he died like a Saint and when his speech failed him ye tears of Devotion streamed down his face with his Eyes Lifted up to Heaven he quited [sic] this miserable World . . . . Many I believe was not sensible how much they esteemed him till he was no more."

Father Herbert Thurston, S.J., produced the Revised Edition of *Butler's Lives*, which appeared in twelve slim volumes (one for the saints of each month of the year) between 1926 and 1938. Thurston, too, paid tribute to the genius of Alban Butler, in an article in the July 1938 issue of *The Month*, an English Catholic periodical: "[Alban Butler] was a friend who inspired trust, a man whose high principles were stimulating to those more worldly or infirm of purpose, a Christian in whom asceticism had not killed human feeling, and a scholar who, in intellectual matters, sought only the truth and never spared himself pains to attain it."

Father Thurston's revised edition was a major rewrite of the original *Butler's*. This was necessitated, he wrote, because "Butler's style, it must be confessed, as judged by modern standards, is deplorably stilted and verbose . . . . Alban Butler as a man, a priest and a scholar, leaves to my thinking, a far more favourable impression than in his character as a writer of English."

Thurston's revised version of Butler's classic work was an immediate hit, and held the field until the appearance of the second edition, in 1956. The work of an English layman, Donald Attwater, this edition eliminated what remained from the first edition—mostly pious homilies better suited to Alban Butler's era. Attwater also cut out some saints whose existence was doubtful. He added others, however, which brought the total to 2,565, compared to Butler's original 1,486.

It is Attwater's second edition, further updated, which is in print today.

There are, of course, dozens of obscure saints in *Butler's*. But obscure does not mean uninteresting—not by a long shot. St. Macedonius (c. A.D. 43), for example, makes a good whimsical candidate for patron saint of good nutrition. "This Syrian ascetic," says *Butler's*, "is said to have lived for 40 years on barley moistened in water till, finding his health impaired, he ate bread, reflecting that it was not lawful for him to shorten his life . . . . This also was the direction he gave to the mother of Theodoret, persuading her, when in a poor state of health, to use proper food, which he said was a form of medicine."

There are numerous saints, of course, who have never been officially canonized, since the canonization process is a relatively late development in Catholic history. *Butler's* is often matter-of-fact about this: "St. Eystein died on January 26, 1188, and in 1229 a synod at Nidaros declared his sanctity. This decree has never been confirmed at Rome, although the preliminary investigations have been begun several times but have always petered out for various reasons."

Too bad, St. Eystein, whoever you are.

Well-known saints get more lengthy treatment in *Butler's*. The articles on St. John Vianney, St. Francis of Assisi, and St. Teresa of Avila, for example, go on for pages. The entry for the Blessed Virgin Mary includes this welcome note of realism: "The Lily of Israel, the Daughter of the princes of Judah, the Mother of all Living, was also a peasant woman, a Jewish peasant woman, the wife of a working man. Her hands were scored with labour, her bare feet dusty, not with the perfumed powder of romance but with the hard stinging grit of Nazareth, of the tracks which led to the well, to the olive gardens, to the synagogue . . ."

The humor in *Butler's* is unmatchable. The reader is regaled as often as he or she is inspired. Of the English reformation martyr, Blessed Edward Waterson (A.D. 1593), we learn: ". . . when Mr. Waterson was tied to the hurdle to be drawn to the place of execution, the horses refused to budge; so he had to be taken to the scaffold on foot, the bystanders saying, 'It would be a vote to the papists which had happened today'; or in modern idiom, 'That's one up for the R.C.'s.'"

It must have been anything but a dull experience to sit for a sermon by the Cure of Ars: "He waged relentless war against blasphemy, profanity and obscenity, and was not afraid to utter from the pulpit the words and expressions that offended God, so there should be no mistake as to what he was talking about."

Stories likely to be of greater inspiration to the modern reader fill many pages in *Butler's*. This description of the home life of St. Thomas More (A.D. 1535) echoes with challenges for the modern family: "All the family and servants met together for night prayers, and at meals a pericope from the Scriptures, with a short commentary, was read aloud by one of the children: this done, discussion and jesting followed . . . . [More] often invited to his table his poorer neighbors, receiving them . . . familiarly and joyously . . ."

Another category is that of marvelous—frequently incredible— wonders and miracles which *Butler's* associates with the lives of many saints. "But," says the author, "among these . . . some legends are beautiful."

One example is from the life of St. Brigid, Abbess of Kildare (c. A.D. 525). Brigid sits with Sister Dara, "a holy nun who was going blind," as the sun is going down. Their conversation so fills their hearts with holy peace that they forget the hour and talk through the night.

As dawn breaks, Brigid is filled with sadness that her companion cannot see the beauty of the sunrise. "So she bowed her head and prayed, and extended her hand and signed the dark orbs of the gentle sister." Sister Dara receives her sight, but is disappointed with what she sees. " 'Close my eyes again, dear Mother, for when the world is so visible to the eyes, God is seen less clearly to the soul.' So Brigid prayed once more, and Dara's eyes grew dark again."

Although the details of many of *Butler's* stories may strike the reader as peculiar, the underlying theme remains that of Christian love, a love willing to undergo great sacrifices for the sake of God and neighbor. Comparisons may be drawn with common inspirational literature, legends of mythical heroes, and skillfully written biography. The critic of literary styles sees woven together in *Butler's* many of the skills of the story-teller's art. A theologian finds on every page living witness to the central truths of Christian faith.

The final word belongs, however, to Donald Attwater (in the July 5, 1957, issue of *Commonweal*): "Some day, perhaps, someone will undertake to write an entirely new Lives of the Saints in English: but he will never be able to forget that he is treading in the steps of Alban Butler."

Contemporary Application

Perhaps Alban Butler decided to write his *Lives of the Saints* because he understood the value of story-telling in the Christian life. As the human authors of the Bible knew, the best way to pass on a faith and a tradition, is to tell stories.

To read stories of the saints, whether ancient or modern, is to join oneself to those down through history in whose lives Christ was most evident. One of the best ways to overcome discouragement and to renew one's commitments, is to read a few stories about saints.

Were Alban Butler alive today, he might well recommend Michael Mott's excellent biography, *The Seven Mountains of Thomas Merton*, or Peter Hebblethwaite's biography of Pope John XXIII. To read such stories is to revitalize one's dedication to living a Christian life in the late 20th century.

Fortunately, our age is able to scrape away the romantic notions about saints that, in the past, often made them seem to have been more than human. These men and women were always human, with the faults and failings of ordinary people. What made them special was their great love, and their willingness to take risks in order to be faithful to their promises.

The saints teach us that a faith that takes no risks is hardly faith at all.

11
Max Picard's *The World Of Silence*

Near the end of World War I, a promising young physician left the University Hospital in Heidelberg, Switzerland, and gave up the practice of medicine. He deserted his profession because he was disillusioned that his colleagues had become fascinated with medical techniques to the point of losing sight of their patients' humanity. The individual person, he felt, had become little more than a guinea pig on which doctors could practice medical mechanics.

The young physician's name was Max Picard. To get a more balanced perspective, Picard studied philosophy, and eventually moved to the tiny village of Caslano, where he lived for virtually the rest of his long life. There he carried out a one-man effort to diagnose the spiritual ills of the 20th century.

Max Picard (1888-1965) was born Jewish. His greatgrandfather had been a rabbi. In 1939, however, Picard converted to Roman Catholicism, and made important contributions to the Swiss Catholic intellectual revival that took place between the end of "the Great War" and the mid-1950s. Picard's two best-known books, *The*

Flight From God, and *The World of Silence*, are written in a remarkable prose-poetry.

The World of Silence was first published in German in 1948. Known to relatively few people today, it has a message that could, given a wide readership, inspire a practical renewal of everyday Christian spirituality undreamed of by its author.

When *The World of Silence* first appeared in English in 1952, Thomas Merton was deeply influenced by it. In the "Author's Note" that prefaced his own slim classic, *Thoughts in Solitude*, Merton wrote: "Those who know Max Picard's stimulating pages in *The World of Silence* will recognize the inspiration of the Swiss philosopher in many of these meditations."

The World of Silence strikes at the heart of the late 20th century's alienation from the spiritual realities in which the human person and all of creation are rooted. For Picard, under, behind, above, below, and in all things there is silence.

The modern world, however, does not understand silence, and so is afraid of it. Not understanding the human need for silence, technological societies drive it away, throw constant blankets of noise over it, and run from the silence as from the abyss.

Still, there is something in the human spirit that requires silence as the body needs food and oxygen. Therefore, the longing for silence is ignored only at the cost of neurosis, psychosis, spiritual starvation, and unhealthy human relationships—a world alienated from its own deepest self. For any human society to ignore its need for silence is to point a gun at its own head, and to slowly, slowly, pull the trigger. Sooner or later, the gun will go off.

The World of Silence consists of an Introduction and thirty-two short meditations on silence in the modern world. Although written in a philosophical style, Picard's meditations are not difficult to follow or understand.

"Silence," Picard begins, "is not simply what happens when we stop talking . . ." Silence is not merely the absence of sound. Rather, a complete world in itself." Silence is always there, behind the talk, behind the noise, waiting to do its healing, nourishing work. Indeed, "Silence belongs to the basic structure of man."

Picard does not suggest that silence is real but words are not. Rather, he insists that human words and conversation depend for their vitality on a communion with silence. Only words born of a communion with silence will benefit the listener. "Language and silence belong together; language has knowledge of silence as silence has knowledge of language."

What is silence? asks Picard. He must depend heavily on analogy and metaphor to respond, for silence embodies a mystery which transcends the human intellect. "There is no beginning to silence, and no end: it seems to have its origins in the time when everything was still pure Being. It is like uncreated, everlasting Being."

One of the central themes of Picard's book is the conviction that silence is feared and rejected by technological societies precisely because it is useless. "Silence is the only phenomenon today that is 'useless.' It does not fit into the world of profit and utility; it simply *is*. It seems to have no other purpose. It cannot be exploited." Anything in the modern world which cannot turn a dollar is virtually without worth.

"Yet," continues Picard, "there is more help and healing in silence than in all the 'useful things' . . . . It makes things whole again, by taking them back from the world of dissipation into the world of wholeness. It gives things something of its own holy uselessness, for that is what silence itself is: holy uselessness."

The World of Silence understands that silence is the remedy for the ills brought on by frantic activity, however well-motivated. Those who hold forth at great length on remedies for stress and burn-out would do well to listen to the simple teaching of Max Picard: "A man in whom the substance of silence is still an active force carries the silence into every movement. His movements are therefore slow and measured. They do not jolt violently against each other; they are borne by the silence; they are simply the waves of silence.

Picard's point is that estranged from silence human nature is unable to remain balanced. "Man is better able to endure things hostile to his own nature, things that use him up, [of which the modern world offers an abundance!] if he has the silent substance within."

Technology in itself, explains Picard, "life with machines, is not injurious unless the protective substance of silence is absent."

There is an intimate relationship between silence and love. Love has more in common with silence than with words. "Nothing interrupts the normal flow of ordinary life so much as love. Nothing takes the world back into silence more than love . . . . In love there is more silence than speech."

So true is this that Christ, the Word of God, the Father's message of love to the world, came from the silence. In a meditation entitled, "World of Myth," the poetic character of Picard's writing is particularly evident:

"Before the coming of Christ, in the final centuries before His birth, a silence went through the ancient world. The old gods were silent, actively silent as an offering to Christ, the God who was coming to men. Now that men no longer sacrificed to the old gods, the gods themselves offered their silence as a sacrifice to the new God. They offered it that He might transform it into the Word."

It is essential to Picard's thought to understand that the mere absence of sound is not identical with true silence. There can be as much noise in a person who is not speaking as in one who is a chatterbox. "Silence must be present within a man as a primary reality in its own right, not merely as the opposite of speech."

Picard insists, however, that what distinguishes human beings from animals is language. People wander from the path of full humanity when words lose contact with silence, when conversation refers only to itself and no longer draws substance and meaning from the sacred well of silence. The person who does not love silence cannot speak out of a full heart. When the silence-language connection is healthy, however, the speaker is a channel of God's grace to others.

Many people, laments Picard using some of his most graphic imagery, have lost the essential human rootedness in silence. "Instead of truly speaking to others today, we are all merely waiting to unload on to others the words that have collected inside us. Speech has become a purely animal, excretive function."

Picard's meditation on "The Radio" is filled with practical applications of his teaching to the modern world. Written just prior to the emergence of television as the dominant medium, much of what he says is easily applied to the ubiquitous tube, as well.

"Radio," writes Picard, "is a machine producing absolute verbal noise. The content hardly matters any longer; the production of noise is the main concern. It is as though words were being ground down by radio, transformed into an amorphous mass . . . And the type of man formed by the constant influence of this noise is the same: formless, undecided inwardly and externally, with no definite limits and standards . . . . There is no more silence, only intervals between radio noises."

No longer, says Picard, do people create radio (and, one might add, television). Rather, radio and TV form people in their own image. The silence is driven away at every opportunity. Today, frequently silence is not even allowed on the telephone. To call a store and be put on "hold" is to be subjected to "canned" music while you wait. Elevators and supermarkets are filled with the same so-called music.

It is, says Max Picard, as if every crack through which silence might seep must be plugged with noises masquerading as sensible sounds. Still, silence remains to be found, and individuals can seek it out to restore spirit, mind, and body.

Max Picard, the former physician, diagnoses the world's disease as a lack of silence. But he does not leave his reader without a prescription for healing. He borrows words from Soren Kierkegaard, the early 19th century Danish Christian philosopher:

"The present state of the world and the whole of life is diseased. If I were a doctor and were asked for my advice, I should reply: Create silence! Bring men to silence. The Word of God cannot be heard in the noisy world of today. And even if it were blazoned forth with all the panoply of noise so that it could be heard in the midst of all the other noise, then it would no longer be the Word of God. Therefore create silence."

Contemporary Application

Granted that silence and quiet are vital to human health and well-being, emotionally, spiritually, and physically, how can we build more quiet into our ordinary lives? There are many opportunities to do this, but they require a willingness to change one's way of life.

One family decided, after a family meeting at which all points of view were heard, that each evening after 9 p.m. would be quiet time. All noise-makers are turned off. No television after 9 o'clock, no radios and no stereo. No kitchen appliances that whir, clatter, or beep. The idea is to allow quiet a chance to emerge and make it easier for people to talk with one another, to read, to study, or pursue some other quiet project.

Single people can easily build into their lives times for quiet and silence. One young woman decided that instead of turning on a morning TV news program she would leave the set off, and prepare to meet the new day quietly, including a few minutes for prayer.

Startled by entering a fast food restaurant to find no canned music coming over the ceiling speakers, a man wrote the management a note saying thanks for the quiet.

Silence and quiet are a rarity in today's world. But they are available to those who take the trouble to seek them out.

12
Thomas Merton's
New Seeds of Contemplation

In 1949, Thomas Merton had been a Trappist monk for eight years, and his autobiography, *The Seven Storey Mountain*, was well on its way to becoming a monumental best-seller. It was 1949 that saw the publication of *Seeds of Contemplation*. Of this early book Merton's biographer, Michael Mott, writes: "For many it remains Merton's finest statement of the spiritual life."

Thirteen years later, in 1962, Merton held in his hands *New Seeds of Contemplation*. In the Preface he had written: "This is not merely a new edition of an old book. It is in many ways a completely new book."

Merton scholar Father William H. Shannon disagrees with Michael Mott. "The most admired of Merton's books on contemplation is, I feel sure, not *Seeds of Contemplation*, but *New Seeds*. Indeed, many students of Merton suspect that *New Seeds of Contemplation* may take its place alongside the great spiritual classics while some of his other books drift into obscurity."

Thirty-nine chapters make up *New Seeds of Contemplation*, and each one stands alone. The reader can easily pick up the book and begin reading any chapter with no sense of disconnectedness. Merton was aware of this, and felt no need to explain himself. In his Author's Note at the beginning of the book, he wrote: ". . . I think a volume of more or less disconnected thoughts and ideas and aphorisms about the interior life needs no particular apology or excuse, even though this kind of book may have become unfamiliar."

Merton points out that works by Pascal, St. John of the Cross, Guigo the Carthusian, and *The Imitation of Christ* are characterized by precisely this style of writing. He disavows, however, any intention on his part to compare his work with masterpieces of spirituality, calling *New Seeds* "nothing more than a collection of notes and personal reflections."

The opening chapter, "What is Contemplation?" shoots material for meditation into the air like quiet fireworks. "Contemplation," writes Merton, ". . . . is spiritual wonder. It is spontaneous awe at the sacredness of life, of being. It is gratitude for being. It is a vivid realization of the fact that life and being in us proceed from an invisible, transcendent and infinitely abundant Source. Contemplation is, above all, awareness of the reality of that Source."

Although there are parts of the book where Merton was not as successful at this as he evidently hoped, he makes clear his intention to speak for everyone, regardless of "state in life." Merton says that "everything that is said here can be applied to anyone, not only in the monastery but also in the world."

"Contemplation," continues Merton, "is also the response to a call: a call from Him Who has no voice, and yet Who speaks in everything that is, and Who, most of all, speaks in the depths of our own being: for we ourselves are words of His."

For the Merton of *New Seeds*, contemplation is an awareness of the transformation brought about by faith. "Contemplation," he says, "is the awareness and realization, even in some sense *experience*, of what each Christian obscurely believes: 'It is now no longer I that live but Christ lives in me.' [Galatians 2:20]."

Merton turns to "What Contemplation is Not," and insists that "contemplation cannot be taught. It cannot even be clearly explained. It can only be hinted at, suggested, pointed to, symbolized."

"Contemplation," writes Merton, "is not trance or ecstasy, nor the hearing of sudden unutterable words, nor the imagination of lights. It is not the emotional fire and sweetness that come with religious exaltation."

Contemplation is also not a sure path to serenity: "Let no one hope to find in contemplation an escape from conflict, from anguish or from doubt . . . genuine contemplation is incompatible with complacency and with smug acceptance of prejudiced opinions . . . Contemplation is no pain killer."

New Seeds of Contemplation is, in a very real sense, a Catholic iconoclast's handbook, encouraging the destruction of false gods on all sides. "So much depends on our idea of God!" exclaims Merton. "Yet no idea of Him, however pure and perfect, is adequate to express Him as He really is."

Then comes the clincher: "Our idea of God tells us more about ourselves than about Him." Thus far a verbal blow to the spiritual solar plexus.

Right away, however, Merton sketches a balanced idea of God that is deceptive in its simplicity: "We must learn to realize that the love of God seeks us in every situation, and seeks our good." Yet risks are necessary in order to be open to this love: "The mind that is the prisoner of conventional ideas, and the will that is the captive of its own desire cannot accept the seeds of an unfamiliar truth and a supernatural desire."

Those today who take Merton's words seriously—and they are words ringing with the truth of God—should prepare themselves to be accused of not playing with a full deck: "My chief care should not be to find pleasure or success, health or life or money or rest or even things like virtue and wisdom—still less their opposites, pain, failure, sickness, death. But in all that happens, my one desire and my one joy should be to know: 'Here is the thing that God has willed for me.'"

That, of course, begs the question. How am I to know the will of God? Merton's response is no easy answer, rather it leaves the reader with the work of prayer and discernment and humility. He insists that "whatever is demanded by truth, by justice, by mercy, or by love must surely be taken to be willed by God."

Merton then plants his thought smack in the good soil of the Scripture's teachings about social justice: "No man who ignores the rights and needs of others can hope to walk in the light of contemplation, because his way has turned aside from truth, from compassion and therefore from God."

Turning to the topic of "detachment," a key idea in traditional Christian spirituality, Merton sets things straight from the start: "We do not detach ourselves from things in order to attach ourselves to God, but rather we become detached *from ourselves* in order to see and use all things in and for God."

Remember, this is the monk who observed the fasts and other disciplines of the monastic life for years, but who also quaffed a beer or two or three whenever he got the chance, who gobbled hamburgers and drank milk shakes with Joan Baez: "There is no evil in anything created by God, nor can anything of His become an obstacle to our union with Him. The obstacle is in our 'self,' that is to say in the tenacious need to maintain our separate, external, egotistic will."

Unintentionally, Merton explains his words and actions best himself: "A saint is capable of loving created things and enjoying the use of them and dealing with them in a perfectly simple, natural manner, making no formal references to God, drawing no attention to his own piety, and acting without any artificial rigidity at all."

New Seeds of Contemplation rides on the crest of a wave from beginning to end. On nearly every page there are thoughts to bring the reader up short, to pause, reflect, pray, or laugh out loud at the nonsensical way he or she lives. "I will never be able to find myself," says Merton, "if I isolate myself from the rest of mankind as if I were a different kind of being."

"Sentences," a chapter made up entirely of aphorisms, all by itself is a work of art. Some samples: "Do not be one of those who, rather than risk failure, never attempts anything."

"If a writer is so cautious that he never writes anything that cannot be criticized, he will never write anything that can be read. If you want to help other people you have got to make up your mind to write things that some men will condemn."

"You cannot be a man of faith unless you know how to doubt. You cannot believe in God unless you are capable of questioning the authority of prejudice, even though that prejudice may seem to be religious."

The final chapter, "The General Dance," includes some of Merton's most poetic prose: "What is serious to men is often very trivial in the sight of God. What in God might appear to us as 'play' is perhaps what He Himself takes most seriously . . . the world and time are the dance of the Lord in emptiness . . . [and] we are invited to forget ourselves on purpose, cast our awful solemnity to the winds and join in the general dance."

Contemporary Application

If there is one word that might be used to describe the spirit of Thomas Merton's *New Seeds of Contemplation,* that word might be "iconoclastic." It's a word that refers to the ancient practice of idol smashing. To be an iconoclast is to shatter false gods. Merton does this with regard to romanticized notions of contemplation, ideas of God, and ideas of spirituality which by-pass relationships with other people.

This iconoclastic tendency in Merton has special value for Catholicism, central to which is the conviction that God is reflected in Creation. Catholicism is convinced that the transcendent, ungraspable

God's love for humankind is more like than unlike the love, for example, of a husband and wife who are lovers as well as friends. God is more like than unlike a beautiful sunset or a beautiful child.

The dark side of this Catholic conviction, however, is the risk that faith may identify the messenger with the Message-Sender, the idea with the Reality. It's good, then, to incorporate a healthy dose of iconoclasm into Christian faith.

My idea of God does not mean God may not be otherwise. The Bible is God's word in human words, not God. Prayer is a means not an end. Religion is not a spiritual tranquilizer.

Faith is fully faith only insofar as it is faith in God alone.

Books For Further Reading

The Imitation of Christ, by Thomas a Kempis. Edited with an Introduction by Harold C. Gardiner, S.J. Doubleday/Image Books.

The Confessions of St. Augustine. Translated with an Introduction by John K. Ryan. Doubleday/Image Books.

Augustine of Hippo, by Peter Brown. University of California Press.

Revelations of Divine Love, by Julian of Norwich. Paulist Press.

Meditations With Julian of Norwich, Introduction and Versions by Brendan Doyle. Bear & Company Books.

The Cloud of Unknowing, Edited and with an Introduction by William Johnston. Doubleday/Image Books.

Francis and Clare: The Complete Works. Paulist Press.

The Divine Comedy of Dante Alighieri, with Translation, Introduction, and Commentary by Allen Mandelbaum. University of California Press, and Bantam Books.

Meditations With Dante Alighieri, Introduction and Versions by James Collins. Bear & Company Books.

Pilgrim in Love: An Introduction to Dante and His Spirituality, by James Collins. Loyola University Press.

The Way of a Pilgrim, and The Pilgrim Continues His Way. Translated by R.M. French. Harper & Row.

Story of a Soul: The Autobiography of St. Therese of Lisieux, Translated by John Clarke, O.C.D. ICS Publications.

The Reed of God, by Caryll Houselander. Christian Classics, Inc.

Caryll Houselander: That Divine Eccentric, by Maisie Ward. Sheed and Ward.

Butler's Lives of the Saints, Edited by Thurston and Attwater. Christian Classics, Inc.

The World of Silence, by Max Picard. Regnery/Gateway, Inc.

New Seeds of Contemplation, by Thomas Merton. New Directions Books.

Thomas Merton: The Development of a Spiritual Theologian, by Donald Grayston. The Edwin Mellen Press.